CANNIBALS

JIMMY LEE SHREEVE

CANNIBALS

TRUE STORIES OF THE HORRIFYING KILLERS WHO FEAST ON HUMAN FLESH

JOHN BLAKE

Published by John Blake Publishing Ltd,
3 Bramber Court, 2 Bramber Road,
London W14 9PB, England

www.johnblakepublishing.co.uk

First published in hardback in 2008
This paperback edition published 2009

ISBN: 978 1 84454 778 4

British Library Cataloguing-in-Publication Data:

A catalogue record for this book is available from the British Library.

Design by www.envydesign.co.uk

Printed in Great Britain by Bookmarque, Croydon CR0 4TD

1 3 5 7 9 10 8 6 4 2

Papers used by John Blake Publishing are natural, recyclable
products made from wood grown in sustainable forests.
The manufacturing processes conform to the environmental
regulations of the country of origin.

To my wife Nicky: 'Like a wildfire and the scent of the night...' And to my two daughters Audra and Imogen, riders on the long lost highway.

Also a big thanks to my sister Lilian, 'Keep the faith.'

In memory of my late father Ted Shreeve (1913–2007), World War II hero and individualist who never let anyone tell him what to do.

'It was like good, fully developed veal, not young, but not yet beef. It was very definitely like that, and it was not like any other meat I had ever tasted...'

William Buehler Seabrook, a *New York Times* reporter talking in 1931 about the taste of human meat after sampling some in the interests of research.

'I' other piece I fried and ate – it was very nice.'

Jack the Ripper, 1888, after sending half a kidney removed from one of his victims to the chairman of the Whitechapel Vigilance Committee

PEOPLE

Many thanks to crime author Carol Anne Davis (www.carolannedavis.co.uk) for sharing her eminently profound insights on cannibal killers. And a big handshake to Jon Tapsell, a fellow author, whose comments made a big difference to this book.

Equal thanks must also go to my agent Andrew Lownie (www.andrewlownie.co.uk), a fine fellow. And thanks also to my editor at Blake, Daniel Bunyard, a good chap who understands that when the werewolf howls there's no turning back...

Plus I must thank my old pal, the movie actor Robert Goodman, for sharing his insights into cannibalism (drawn from his experience as a method actor). And a big cheers to my friend Canadian shaman Dr Crazywolf (www.wolfshaman.com) for adding an unexpected element to this title.

Appreciation is also due to my friend Martin Bradsworth for providing the necessary fine gin and rum and other medicines required to write even a sentence. I'm sure we also discussed the subject matter of this book, but I can't remember any of it...

Lastly, a very big thanks to my wife Nicky for her seriously excellent copyediting which, as usual, saved the day!

SOFTWARE

* FireFox web browser and Thunderbird email application – both open source (free) from www.mozilla.com
* WriteItNow – novel and non-fiction writing software from www.ravensheadservices.com
* AeroPlayer – if you use a Palm handheld like I do this is a great alternative to the iPod. Truly excellent bass response. From www.aerodrome.us

ROCK AND ROLL

Ian Hunter (particularly his latest album *Shrunken Heads*), whose lyrics and music have inspired me since I was a boy in Northampton. And Status Quo, who are seriously back on form with their latest album *In Search of the Fourth Chord*; along with the brilliant *Raising Sand* from Robert Plant and Alison Krauss. Plus digital radio station *Planet Rock* (www.planetrock.co.uk), my essential listening.

CONTENTS

INTRODUCTION

Just over two years ago I came into contact with a cannibal. Thankfully he wasn't a killer. In fact, he was oddly non-violent. He had managed to keep any homicidal tendencies at bay throughout his life. He told me he satisfied his desire for human flesh by cutting pieces off newly dead bodies obtained (illegally) from mortuaries or from cemeteries.

The disturbing and intensely shocking discussions I had with him via email and instant messaging led me to write this book. I wanted to know why he and others like him developed, or were born with, a desire to eat human flesh. The guy I communicated with assured me he had never killed or harmed anyone. But many with cannibalistic inclinations have murdered innocent victims to feast on their flesh.

In October 1982, for example, Japanese student Issei Sagawa, who had a near genius-level IQ, invited his Dutch girlfriend to dinner at his Paris flat. What he didn't tell her was that she was on the menu as the main course.

Once inside the flat, Sagawa shot her in the neck with his rifle, cut up her body, cooked her and ate her. He even took photographs as he dismembered her and tape-recorded their last moments together.

Then in 2001, in Fort Worth, Texas, Joey Cala (forty-one) beat his 79-year-old mother to death, cut her open and ate some of her heart. Police found him standing over his mother Lydia's body, blood dripping from his mouth. By all accounts he looked like a hyena after a feeding frenzy at a carcass. A medical examiner later testified that Cala most likely bludgeoned his mother to death with his bare hands, before cutting open her chest and abdomen and removing some of her organs.

Cala had been living with his mother since being paroled from a drink driving conviction in December 2000. He had also served time for drug possession and aggravated assault on a public servant.

Forensic psychologist Dr Kelly Goodness said Cala appeared to suffer from schizophrenia and had been on medication.

Clearly, Cala must have been severely disturbed to have been capable of killing his mother and then eating sections of her heart. It's an act most of us would have extreme difficulty even to contemplate.

Saying that, few of us could imagine eating the flesh from a body that has passed away legitimately – as my cannibal confidant claimed to have done. The chilling thing was he appeared to be perfectly sane, save for his predilection for eating human flesh.

CANNIBALS

Because I've got a long-time background in magic and the occult, I can't help but wonder if there is some esoteric precedent for cannibalism. Could it be that those who eat human flesh – be they murderers or eaters of legitimately dead corpses – are responding to some primal urge? Could such an urge be programmed deep into our DNA? Could it be that certain circumstances or mental states bring it out?

Although anthropologists have squabbled for years over whether cannibalism exists or not, they now agree that it is a tradition that spans cultures and centuries. The term cannibalism derives from the name of the West Indian Carib tribe. They were first documented by the explorer Christopher Columbus and allegedly ate other humans in religious rites.

Besides religious sacrifice, the Aztecs are believed to have carried out cannibalism on a large scale as part of the ritual killing of war captives, in a practice known as 'exocannibalism' – the eating of strangers or enemies.

Aborigines in Australia are thought to have practised a more benevolent form of cannibalism – known as 'endocannibalism' – which involves the consumption of friends and relatives who have died of natural causes and have not been specially slaughtered for eating. The dead were ritually eaten as a means of allowing their spirits to live on.

The Maori of New Zealand also ate human flesh. Dead relatives were consumed in solemn funeral rites, while enemies were carved up, cooked and eaten to ingest their fighting spirit and guile.

All this might seem primitive and barbaric. But there are other ways of looking at it. One old Maori, quoted in late Victorian times, said: 'When you die, wouldn't you rather be eaten by your own kinsmen than by maggots?'

He had a point. What's more, it could be argued that if cannibalism were still socially acceptable, and we still ate our dead relatives like the Maoris did, then cannibalistic killings might be very rare or non-existent – as the perpetrators' appetites would be satisfied.

This would undoubtedly have been the case with Armin Meiwes, whose taste for human flesh shocked the world in 2001. His yearning to cannibalise someone led to him advertising on websites for 'young, well-built men aged eighteen to thirty to slaughter'.

Amazingly, he got a taker – one Bernd-Jurgen Brandes. Meiwes told investigators that he took Brandes back to his home in Germany. There, Brandes agreed to have his penis cut off (something he'd fantasised about for years), which Meiwes then flambéed and served up for them both to eat. Meiwes said he then killed Brandes with his full consent and ate 44 pounds of his flesh.

It's hard to believe that either man could have been sane. Meiwes certainly had an overbearing and tyrannical mother, which must have taken its psychological toll and been at the root of his strange desires. But Dr George Stolpmann, who did the preliminary psychological report on the forty-two-year-old Meiwes, said there was 'no evidence of a psychological disorder'. He admitted, however, that Meiwes did have a 'schizoid personality'.

Brandes also appeared to have been mentally stable. His father insisted that his son had never shown any signs of depression; nor had there been any evidence that he entertained morbid or suicidal thoughts. Brandes' last lover agreed. But one earlier sex partner alleged that Brandes had offered him 10,000 marks to bite off his penis.

CANNIBALS

If Brandes and Meiwes weren't deranged, the best you can say is neither man shared the same reality tunnel on life and death as the majority of us.

Chillingly, their mindset may not be as rare as we would like to think. Rudolf Egg, a criminologist with the German Central Criminal Service, says cannibalism has always been around and shows no sign of dying out. 'There are several hundred people with cannibalistic tendencies here in Germany alone,' he warns, 'and many thousands around the world.'

If he is right, it's only a matter of time before someone else with a taste for human flesh reaches for the carving knife...

ONE:

ENTER THE
DEATH EATER

It was spring 2007 when I first came into contact with the cannibal. He told me his name was Eric Soames. I'm pretty sure this wasn't his real name. Considering his macabre tastes and his apparent good standing in life, it was unlikely he would have come clean with his true identity.

He got in touch with me after reading my *Doktor Snake's Voodoo Spellbook* (St Martin's Press 2004), which has become a cult classic. The book cemented my reputation as an expert on voodoo and the occult.

This reputation was the reason Soames contacted me. He felt he needed informed advice on a difficult, not to say terrifying, matter, which involved both unnatural desires and the occult.

When Soames' email dropped into my inbox I took one scan of it and thought, 'Another crazyhead'. But for some reason or other I didn't delete it, and found myself reading it a couple of hours later.

This is what the message said:

From: Eric Soames <soamese733@XXXXXX.com>
Subject: A delicate problem – can you help?
Dear Mr. Shreeve,
Can I talk to you about a problem I have? It would need to be in the strictest confidence as the matter is not only very delicate but could prove incriminating.

I would understand if you do not wish to pursue this any further.
The reason I have come to you is I have read both your books – 'Blood Rites' and 'Doktor Snake' – from cover to cover and I am in no doubt that you are one of the world's leading experts on the occult and strange phenomena. It is also clear that you have personally practised the occult arts.

Believe me when I tell you I would not have contacted you if I wasn't desperate.

You see I have, for want of a better word, an affliction. It is as terrifying as it is foul. It makes me feel rotten to the core. I am a vile and bestial monster.

Yet I strongly believe that my vileness is down to 'external influences'.
This is where you come in. I want someone of your calibre in the occult world to assess my condition and give me an informed opinion as to whether the evil that I am comes from within or without.

I believe you may be my only hope. I have consulted a number of leading psychiatrists to no avail.

2

CANNIBALS

I am a successful businessman. So I can certainly pay you. Please name your fee.

Thank you for your time.

Yours sincerely,

Eric Soames.

While the offer of a fee had its appeal (there are few writers who can afford to turn down the offer of greenbacks), it seemed certain that Soames was nothing more than a literate nutcase. So I didn't reply.

But then, a couple of days later, another email dropped into my inbox. This time Soames laid his cards on the table. His revelations chilled me to the bone. To say I was shocked and utterly repelled by the man's depravity would be an understatement – and I've been a journalist for nearly twenty years.

Soames told me he had an extremely strong, almost uncontrollable, inclination toward cannibalism – or 'anthropophagy' (the urge to eat humans) as it is known in academic circles.

Unlike serial killers with cannibalistic tendencies, Soames hadn't actually murdered anyone to satisfy his needs. But he was frightened that one day he would no longer be able to resist killing someone in cold blood to satisfy his hunger.

This was why he wanted to consult me. He thought I might be able to help him discover why he had cannibalistic urges, and perhaps find a way to keep them at bay, or even exorcise them altogether.

Soames believed he was possessed by a demon, a monstrous

atavism from the primal swamp – 'an entity utterly cold toward humanity because it preceded us by an eternity'.

Whether this was a metaphor for serious underlying psychological problems was difficult to say. But Soames did have a very difficult childhood.

'Both my parents used to beat me for the slightest things,' he said in his email to me. 'One word or even look out of place and my father would take his belt to me. My mother would look on, relishing it. Once she told him to take a kitchen knife to me – "Let's see the colour of his vile, disobedient blood", she said. So he did. He cut a small chunk out of my arm, from which flowed a stream of blood. Like the witch that she was my mother shrieked with hysterical laughter.'

These cruel punishments went on regularly – despite the fact that his parents were staunch church-goers.

Then at twelve years old, in a fit of despair, Soames went down to the bottom of the garden where he couldn't be seen and recited the Lord's Prayer backwards. He'd heard somewhere that this summons the Devil himself. He'd increasingly come to identify with the Bible's arch bad guy. His reasoning was this: if his parents summed up the Godly then the other side – Satan and his fallen angels – had to be a better bet.

All Soames could recall of his evocation of Satan was a bleak, sickening feeling that he was unleashing forces far beyond his control. These, he felt, would one day consume him. In fact, such was his terror that he passed out on reaching 'heaven in art which Father Our', the final line of the Lord's Prayer recited backwards.

Shortly after this incident Soames started to get urges to

consume blood. He fantasised about killing his mother and father and eating them. He would look at his school friends and imagine drugging them and slicing flesh from their thighs, cooking it up and consuming it.

'I was at once disgusted and repelled, but at the same time there was a feeling of unimaginable elation,' he recalled. 'It was to the point that I had an uncontrollable erection and had to masturbate, otherwise I felt I might explode.'

But somewhere, deep inside himself, Soames had morality. He did not want to harm a living soul to satisfy his unnatural needs.

Eventually it occurred to him that he didn't need to kill to fulfil his craving for human flesh. All he had to do was go to a mortuary or graveyard and take a slice off a freshly dead person. So long as he wasn't caught and the relatives didn't find out, this would hurt no one, he reasoned.

'I got my first human flesh from a local mortuary,' Soames confided to me. 'I literally spent weeks staking the place out to discover a way of getting in and out without being seen.'

Once he was satisfied he could do this, Soames went into the mortuary with a razor-sharp carving knife in his satchel bag.

'I had to be quick. The attendant was having a cigarette break, as he invariably did around 4:30pm,' he recalled. 'My heart pounding, I dashed in and found the corpse of a middle-aged woman on the slab. I remember her thighs were huge and reminded me of legs of pork. So I sliced a chunk off both, then a small section from her left breast, and dropped them into a plastic bag, which I concealed in my satchel.'

After having got out without being seen, Soames dashed home.

'I knew my mother and father would not return for a

couple of hours, so I put the woman's meat in a pan and fried it in butter,' Soames related. 'I masturbated as the meat cooked. When I reached orgasm I let the semen drip into the pan.'

By his own admission, Soames gobbled up the human flesh like a 'ravenous wolf'.

Since that day, every few months or so, Soames has satisfied his desire for human flesh by eating small sections cut from the dead. 'I'm a death eater,' he once said in his communications to me.

At first I thought Soames must be a vermin-like specimen of humanity living on the fringes of society. Far from it. He is a successful businessman selling a range of New Age products and services. Or, at least, that is what he told me during our correspondence. I have no reason to doubt him. If nothing else Soames' literate writing style tends to back up his claim that, apart from his cannibalistic inclinations, he is a normal member of society.

The fact that Soames couldn't be identified in a crowd as being weird in some way aroused my curiosity. It was the main reason I decided to communicate with him. Even though he offered it, I didn't take a fee from him. Instead I decided to write a book about cannibalism – this book.

To his credit Soames said he had not harmed anyone – yet – to fulfil his desires. Unlike some, who murder the innocent solely to eat their flesh. Regrettably cannibal killers are not rare. They crop up in the news all too regularly.

The question I wanted an answer to was why people do it. Are they born with a desire to kill and eat human flesh? Or do social and environmental circumstances lead them down such a macabre path in life?

CANNIBALS

As far as Soames is concerned, the answer is simple. The physical abuse he received from his parents as a child not only damaged him psychologically, it opened up his psyche enough to allow an external force – what he believed was a demonic entity – to enter and possess him.

Unsurprisingly, criminal psychologists have little or no time for explanations rooted in the occult. It's not part of their remit. They prefer to cite childhood abuse or psychological traumas as being the sole causes of deviant behaviour. But in quite a number of cases of cannibalistic killing there is little or no sign of an abused childhood or emotional disturbances.

I like to keep an open mind and neither believe nor disbelieve anything. I'm prepared to assess both scientific and occult theories and test them against the facts. In some respects my perspective is unique. As well as my long-time background in magic and the occult, I've also spent many years writing science and technology articles for national newspapers.

This is why I didn't dismiss Soames's claims of demonic possession. I'm not saying I believe in the objective reality of demons; what I am saying is I think the human mind is a far bigger 'universe' in itself than most of us – even psychologists – give it credit for.

As Zen Buddhism has it: there's the 'little mind', which is the conscious, everyday part of our mind and runs the internal chatter and rational thought processes. Behind that is the 'big mind', which is the vast reservoir of the unconscious. In this aspect of our psyche are the gods, angels and demons... the beautiful dreams, primal memories, UFOs, the Loch Ness monster and the yeti...

7

along with the vilest of fantasies and depraved lusts. Some of which, given the right circumstances, can consume and obsess us. If our grip on consensus, or agreed, reality happens to be tenuous, there is a worrying chance we will act on them...

This could be what happens with cannibals, both when they kill and when they raid mortuaries and graveyards to gratify their need for human flesh. They could be responding to a primal memory – embedded deep in their unconscious or DNA – of a time when cannibalism was acceptable or even the norm as part of funeral rites. As anthropologists now state, cannibalism has been practised in all cultures at one time or another down the centuries.

But I should make one thing clear when I speak of the unconscious mind and the dreams and imaginative processes that spring from it. None of it should necessarily be considered any less 'real' than the workings of the conscious mind. Just because the unconscious operates in the realm of metaphor and dreams doesn't mean it isn't there. After all, its influence on everyday reality can be felt. Especially if someone acts on their more extreme or deranged fantasies.

This is what may have happened in 2001 when Armin Meiwes placed his advert on the internet. Was he acting on the violent, macabre and gory fantasies that had lived vividly in his psyche since childhood?

TWO:
SICK LOVE

KID CANNIBAL

As a boy, Armin Meiwes' favourite TV programme was Flipper. This wasn't because he liked to watch the antics of the friendly dolphin that starred in the 1960s children's adventure series. It was because he wanted to eat the dolphin's owner, Sandy.

The young TV star was Meiwes' ideal: blonde, fit and outgoing. Sandy summed up everything the introverted, maternally dominated Meiwes wanted to be. He felt that by eating him, he would take on Sandy's characteristics and become just like him.

It was a macabre form of self-improvement born of an imaginative child. With hindsight, of course, you could say Meiwes was deranged as well as imaginative. But the truth is that such an idea has its precedents. Ritualistic forms of cannibalism, for example, strongly mirror

Meiwes' ideas; you eat someone you aspire to and inherit their characteristics.

While this might sound like the logic of primitive barbarians, it has been practised as recently as 2002. A rebel group in the Democratic Republic of the Congo launched a vicious offensive against Pygmy tribes in the eastern Congo. This involved killing and eating many of the unfortunate tribespeople. One source said the rebel soldiers even 'sprinkled salt on the flesh as they ate'. The prevailing theory holds that the soldiers ate the Pygmies in order to absorb their unique forest powers – good vision, endurance and tracking skills.

Clearly, Meiwes might have had unusual ideas as a boy, but they weren't that unusual. Certainly not when you look at the varied beliefs and practices of cultures from around the world. Okay, thirty years later, his fantasies took him over and he killed a man and ate 20kg of his flesh, including his penis, in a bloody and gruesome cannibalistic rite. But Meiwes was not violent. The slaughter was done with the full permission of the victim. Strictly speaking it was not murder. And when you look at Meiwes' life he certainly didn't show any signs of being violent or even aggressive. Yes, his fantasies revolved around such themes. But it seemed he wouldn't harm a fly unless the fly made it very clear that it was turned on by the idea of being squished.

The bottom line is: if you had a choice between spending a day or two with Meiwes or a Saturday night in one of Britain's city or town centres, you'd be well advised to opt for the former. Meiwes just didn't hurt people unless they gave him their full consent. Whereas the brutish young drunks that populate our town centres at weekends think nothing of beating people half to death or stabbing them. Sometimes they kill.

Yet they run loose, while Meiwes languishes in jail...

Meiwes was born on 1 December 1961. He spent his early childhood in Essen-Holsterhausen in the Ruhr industrial area of West Germany. His mother, Waltraud, had been married before and he had two half-brothers from that relationship. Meiwes' father, Dieter, was a policeman, some nineteen years younger than his wife.

Life wasn't easy for Dieter and Waltraud – they had many ups and downs. They kept going as best they could and even bought a thirty-room, rambling farmhouse near Rotenburg for family holidays.

In the end though, Dieter and Waltraud separated. Dieter left the family home, taking one of Meiwes' brothers with him, while the other was sent to live with his biological father in Berlin. He decided it would be best if the young Armin stayed with his mother.

Whether this decision was the one that put Armin on the route to having overwhelming cannibalistic desires is open to debate. Would things have turned out differently if Armin had gone to live with his father instead of staying with his mother?

Who knows? What is certain is his mother Waltraud turned him into a virtual servant who had to obey all her rules and wishes. There was no room for youthful rebellion. He had to clean the silverware till it shone like a mirror, wash the dishes, put the rubbish out and endless other chores.

Worse still, she made him wear traditional Bavarian-style

lederhosen to school. It was the beginning of the 1970s. All the other boys were wearing flared jeans to school. Unsurprisingly, he didn't fit in and became a figure of fun.

What's more, he was isolated. His father and two brothers had gone. Where once he had a family... brothers to confide in and the masculine balance of a father... now he just had his mother. It wouldn't have been so bad if she had been more easygoing. Unfortunately, she wouldn't even let Armin go out to play with his friends. He had his household chores to do.

The only respite he had was visiting a local farm to watch the animals being slaughtered. By all accounts he took great enjoyment in watching the pigs, ducks, hens and geese being dispatched.

In the end, like many children who feel lonely and isolated, Armin created an imaginary friend. He was called Franky and Armin was able to confide in him and tell him his secrets – the kind of things he would have told his brothers had they still lived with him. The question is, was Franky another sign of Armin developing pathological thinking patterns?

Probably not. The latest research reveals that invisible playmates – the mysterious characters that take up residence in family homes – are very beneficial to children. A study from the Institute of Education in London found that they offer companionship, emotional support, aid creativity, boost self-esteem and create a 'sense of self'.

The upshot of the study was that parents have no cause to worry even if their child dreams up a whole host of invisible companions. 'Imaginative children will create imaginary friends,' says Karen Majors, an educational psychologist at the Institute who is conducting the research.

During our correspondence, Eric Soames – the non-homicidal cannibal – and I discussed the Armin Meiwes case. He concurred that invisible playmates can be highly beneficial for children. 'But not all invisible friends are part of the child's psyche, some come from outside,' he said. He was referring to poltergeists, supposedly discarnate spirits that disrupt people's lives or even possess them. One of the worst case scenarios of this was depicted in *The Exorcist* movie, in which a young girl was completely overtaken by a discarnate entity known as Pazuzu, the terrifying and malevolent wind devil of Assyrian and Babylonian legend. It made her scream and shout, levitate, utter profanities and masturbate with a crucifix. Both the movie and original book of the same name were fictional. But in personal correspondence with me, the book's author, William Peter Blatty, made clear it was based on a true story concerning the reported possession of a young boy who, at one stage, nearly killed the Catholic priests attempting to exorcise him.

Eric Soames believed that Franky was of this nature, an evil spirit with a penchant for eating human flesh. He also voiced suspicions that Franky could have been an ancient atavism or demon from the primal pit – possibly Pazuzu, which was described by cult author William S. Burroughs in *Cities of the Red Night* (1981) as 'Lord of Fevers and Plagues, Dark Angel of the Four Winds with rotting genitals from which he howls through sharpened teeth over stricken cities?'

'You have to remember,' said Soames, 'that Armin Meiwes

was looking at his classmates like you might look at a succulent pork chop in a butcher's shop. His mouth watered with hunger. This is not natural by any stretch of the imagination, as I can personally attest. Psychologists insisting such desires are down to an abused childhood is all well and good, but it doesn't explain the sheer depravity of it all.'

As far as Soames was concerned demon possession offers a model to explain the unbelievable horror of cannibalism.

I pointed out that many people would see this as an archaic, unsophisticated way of looking at deviant behaviour.

'With our modern-day rationalism we con ourselves into thinking we have the answers for everything and that people in the past were ignorant savages – it's imperialism in the extreme,' Soames replied. 'But how do we know they weren't seeing the bigger reality? Can we not accept that they might have been on to something?'

Although I am no stranger to ritual magic and Voodoo, which often involves spirit possession, I tend to think much of what might seem outside the mind – like spirits and demons – are really inside the huge universe of the human psyche. But when you look at Armin Meiwes' desire to eat people it's hard to see him as human; the baleful presence of something demonic seems to always be lurking in the shadows.

Take Armin's favourite childhood story, Hansel and Gretel, for example. The section he read again and again was where the witch 'fattens up little Hansel' in the hope of cooking and eating him. Armin used to act out this scene regularly, playing the role of the witch and relishing the idea of roasting and devouring Hansel.

Unsurprisingly, he went on to enjoy gruesome horror movies that involved bodies being ripped apart with the resultant exposure of organs and entrails. Blood and gore became Armin's porn, and reinforced the anchoring of cannibalism and death to his burgeoning sexuality.

By the age of twelve, and the onset of puberty, he would masturbate while fantasising about feasting on the body of another boy. Girls didn't appeal to him in this way. He believed they were too important to kill as they were essential for propagating the race (male sperm, he reasoned, could be frozen and artificially inseminated into women to keep up population levels).

In 1977, Armin and his mother left Essen and moved to their rambling seventeenth-century holiday farmhouse, near Rotenburg.

It was a dark, foreboding building, in poor repair. It looked like the Munsters' house rather than a Wimpey home, which was why local kids called it the 'haunted house'.

Waltraud stoically ignored such jibes and called it her 'estate'. She considered herself upper-middle-class – or at least this was what she aspired to. Because of this she saw herself as above menial toil, and therefore didn't work. Unfortunately, she didn't have the cash to back this up; she and Armin subsisted off the rent Waltraud charged for the property they had left behind in Essen.

Waltraud couldn't afford servants, which would have been the mark of an upper-middle-class lifestyle. So she used Armin instead. He had to make the beds, polish the silverware, wash the dishes and clean the floors. Waltraud mercilessly dominated him and bossed him around. Woe betide him if he shirked his duties.

Neighbours felt sorry for him. They wondered why he didn't go out and spend time with boys his own age, or chase girls. None suspected he had strong homosexual leanings.

At a local village party, neighbours shook their heads when Waltraud reprimanded the sixteen-year-old Armin: 'Armin, don't hold your cutlery like that,' she chided. 'Make sure you're holding your knife and fork with your fingers in the correct position. You naughty boy.'

THE WITCH

Because of his strange desire to taste human flesh, Armin didn't fit into the mainstream. He stood outside society. In a sense he was a rebel (although not towards his mother) whose fantasies pitted him against everything so-called 'decent' people stood for. This may have been why he took to the witch who lived next door to the farmhouse.

Both Waltraud and Armin used to visit Ulla von Bernus, who had moved there in 1968, almost every day. They all became great pals.

Ulla, however, wasn't keen on being described as a witch. She preferred to call herself a priestess of Satan. Her real name was Dannenberge, but she thought 'von Bernus' had a more glamorous ring to it. In keeping with her dark image, Ulla painted the walls of her house black and hung pictures of Lucifer everywhere. The centrepiece of the lounge was an altar to Satan, complete with black mirror, dagger and candles. Just in case anyone was in any doubt, the doorbell on the front door (again painted black) was a skull, out of which popped a tongue. It was the kind of occult kitsch that heavy metal outfits would popularize.

Local kids called her farmhouse the 'witch's house'. You could hardly blame them. But if nothing else Ulla added colour to the village. She would often be seen with a Dunhill cigarette hanging from her deep red lips, fingers heavy with rings, in deep conversation with Waltraud and waving her hands manically as she emphasised the points she was making.

A divorcee, she held regular Satanic masses and claimed to be able to curse people to death.

'I kill whenever Satan orders,' she said, claiming she nearly always succeeded. 'I have a ninety per cent success rate.'

Hexing was part of her occult business. She charged between 300 and 1,000 German marks to get rid of people in fatal car crashes or falling downstairs. Her clientele was typically desperate women who wanted to bump off unfaithful husbands. These were people who had little power in life and so magic offered them an opportunity to match or even better their husbands, many of whom could well have been planning to get off lightly when it came to divorce settlements.

By all accounts, Ulla was inundated with calls from women – and some men – throughout Germany keen to wreak revenge on straying spouses. But Ulla was choosy about her clients. She would only lay a death curse on people who deserved it, like sex criminals.

'I am categorically in favour of the death penalty,' she said. 'I have sent twenty men to eternal damnation via a ritual distance killing. I bewitched them to death. And each time I made it look like an accident.'

She also used magic to reunite and separate lovers, and solve other problems.

'My hexes and spell casting are superior to all others,' she said in her advertising materials. 'I can help you achieve anything you want; just tell me what you need done and through my extremely powerful spell work it will be done immediately. I get the job done using my own method of black magic. Come to me with any problem and be rid of it tomorrow.'

Her reputation rocketed when three judges heading a court case suffered from heart attacks and the prosecutor was fatally injured. The accused, a child molester, had once been a neighbour of Ulla and it was presumed she had used her powers to help him. In reality, this was unlikely to have been the case – unless she truly believed he was innocent. She hated sex criminals.

Ulla made national headlines in the 1980s when she was taken to court by an unhappy customer who had paid her 3,000 marks to lay a death hex on her husband, who didn't die. The court eventually ruled that von Bernus was guilty of an 'illusory crime exempt from punishment' and ordered her to pay the money back.

Ulla was also a regular at the roulette table in Bad Harzburg, but she hardly ever won – Satan, she said, had better things to do than help her in her quest for wealth.

As a teenager, Armin was gripped by Ulla's tales and stories. She'd tell him how she was in contact with extraterrestrials and how her 'vision quests' brought her into communication with anthropomorphic beings with cloven hooves, barbed tails and horns. 'Atlantis is going to reappear, but the world will soon disappear into chaos,' she would say.

Ulla's ambition was to appear on a talk show with the

Pope to discuss it all. She believed humans are animals (which, of course, we are) and that we should accept our nature and not see ourselves as above any other animals. As far as she was concerned Satan was the dark force in nature and she wanted him to usurp God. It's hard to imagine the Pope being overjoyed at such an idea...

But it would be too easy to dismiss Ulla as evil. In fact, the Satanic path is a perfectly acceptable and beneficial path in life. You could certainly argue that it is a good deal less hypocritical than Christianity. Satanism accepts us for what we are – animals that can think and reason – but unlike Christianity it never puts us above any other creature on this earth.

This is why I don't accept that Ulla was necessarily a bad influence on Armin – despite the claims of the popular press, which has little understanding of the occult. In fact I'd go as far as saying she was a good influence on the teenager. Besides regaling him with fantastic and colourful stories and ideas, she provided the friendship that he was so sadly lacking in.

In 1986, due to money problems, Ulla was forced to move away.

Eventually, Armin's strange cannibalistic fantasies started to grip him more and more. They demanded some level of physical manifestation, as many vivid fantasies do. Armin started to act out his inner visions. He would dismember Barbie dolls and cook up their severed limbs on the barbecue in the garden. He then moved on to making his own dolls out of marzipan. He also moulded the marzipan into the shape of a penis, heart, liver and stomach, and ate them. At night he used pork and tomato ketchup to simulate scenes of mutilated flesh covered in blood.

He took photos and videos of his grizzly work, but carefully locked these away so his mother wouldn't see them.

None of this stopped him leading an apparently normal life outside the home. He worked hard at school and when he left at eighteen with good exam results, he joined the army. He was ideally suited to military life as he was used to being ordered around by his mother. Unlike his peers he would turn up ten minutes early for shifts and even volunteered for extra shifts. He joined as a non-commissioned officer in ordnance, but soon moved up the ranks due to being so conscientious.

His battalion was stationed in Rotenburg, which meant he could go home to his mother every night. When he was required to go on troop outings, Waltraud simply went with him and they shared a double room. Not surprisingly, his army pals found this very strange. 'Armin, you're such a mama's boy,' teased one of the officers. 'Does she make you wash behind your ears before you go to bed? Do you have to ask her permission to go to the toilet too? Don't you think you're old enough to spend a night away from your mummy? Good God, man, you're not seven anymore.'

Armin didn't let this kind of thing get to him. He was oblivious to it.

On the rare occasions he dated women, his mother insisted on tagging along. Waltraud would sit in the back of the car listening to the conversation. It must have been excruciatingly embarrassing for all concerned – though perhaps Armin and his mother considered it normal. Either way, Waltraud was not impressed with any of the women Armin went out with.

'She's not good enough for you, Armin,' she would say. 'You can't be seen with someone as common as that. Did you hear the way she talked? Her enunciation is atrocious.'

Armin took care not to introduce Waltraud to his male friends – she'd have hit the roof if she got wind of his homosexual leanings.

In 1991, Armin left the army and retrained as a computer technician. Once qualified, it didn't take him long to find a job with a software firm. His hard-working nature and dedication shone through. He enjoyed his job and for the next few years things went well. He was earning good money, which allowed him to indulge himself by buying lots of computer equipment and old cars to do up (but he tended to leave these to rust in the garden). He also spent his cash on good suits, which meant he was always smartly turned out.

But on 2 September 1999, Armin's world turned upside down. After a long illness his mother died. She was seventy-seven. Armin was devastated. She might have bossed him around all the time and mercilessly dominated him but, although flawed, she was his world, his rock.

'It's terrible. Now I'm alone in the world,' he told work colleagues.

The feeling of being alone in the world was so intense for Armin he started imagining he was his mother. One day he gave an old school friend a shock when he opened the door to him dressed in his mother's floral frock, makeup and wig.

It was like a real-life re-run of Alfred Hitchcock's *Psycho*, only no one spotted the parallels until it was too late...

WILLING VICTIM

After his mother's death, Armin started researching cannibalism. He was heartened to discover that most cultures have practised it at one time or another over the centuries, and that it was seen as an acceptable way to recycle the bodies of dead friends and relatives.

Getting an internet connection proved a big boon. It allowed him to download thousands of pornographic pictures of violence, torture and cannibalism. He also hung out in hardcore chat rooms including Cannibal Cafe, Gourmet Guy Cannibals, TortureNet and DolcettGirls. Here humans were described as 'long pigs', a reference to the fact that human meat is said to be similar in taste to pork. Subjects discussed included people's preferences for slaughter and how to practise 'safe cannibalism'.

Armin regularly visited around 430 cannibal websites and chat rooms. He even set up his own chat room on Yahoo! Here he published his own stories and views, and encouraged online exchanges.

One man told Armin during a chat room conversation that he liked to go to slaughterhouses and imagine it was humans being killed. The online cannibalism world was not short of would-be victims either. Someone with the screen name 'Helleater' told Armin he dreamt of 'being BBQed on a large grill (till it's so hot for me)'. While Lisa, whose online nickname was 'Snuffy', said she was 'looking for a real sadist and cannibal, who will torture me over a long period, things like cutting off my toes and fingers... remove

my teeth, that I can't bite you... And much, much more.'
The twenty-two-year-old said she could 'travel everywhere
to have her desires met'.

One message from a Dane with the screen name 'Tufke'
really hooked Armin's interest.

'If anyone wants to eat an eighteen-year-old gorgeous
male by any means you wish,' wrote Tufke, 'just tell me how
you would feel whilst devouring my horny flesh into ur belly
and i will reply to you so we can discuss real arrangements,
please eat me!'

Armin, who wasn't too hot with his English, replied under
his screen name 'Franky', the name of his boyhood imaginary
friend.

'Hi, I am Franky from Germany. I will eat you. Please tell
me your height and weight, also send me a pic from you.
Where are you from? I hope you can come quick to me, I am
a hungry cannibal. Your butcher, Franky.'

Next, Armin posted sixty adverts in the personal columns of
cannibal forums, again using his pseudonymn 'Franky' and
the email address 'antrophagus@hotmail.com'. Antrophagus
meant cannibal and was taken from the Greek term for
human flesh eating 'anthropophagos'.

Armin's ads had titles like 'Search for a young boy' or
'Search boys for butchering'. One read:

I am Franky from Germany and i search for a young
Boy, between 18 and 30 y/o. Have you a normal build
body and will you di, then come to me, i butchering you
and eat your horny flesh.

Amazingly, Armin got 204 replies from people offering themselves for slaughter and consumption. He got a further thirty offering to do the slaughtering and fifteen simply wanting to watch.

After corresponding with applicants he set up some thirty meetings, some of which led to him travelling as far afield as the Netherlands. All fell through. It was one thing fantasising anonymously on the internet, but quite another thing doing it for real.

In July 2000, things started to look up. Armin got to know 'Jörg' from Villingen, Schwenningen, a thirty-one-year-old hotel cook who fantasised about being killed and eaten. Jörg went to visit Armin. Once preliminary coffee and small talk was done with, Armin tied him up and used a coloured pen to mark the best cuts of meat on his body, much like a butcher would on a meat carcass.

Jörg went along with it all – until it got serious. He complained that his ankles hurt and said no. Armin tried over and over again to persuade him to let him slaughter him. But got nowhere. Jörg finally admitted he only wanted to act out cannibalistic fantasies because it turned him on. He didn't want to carry them out in reality.

Armin let him go. He only wanted to kill a willing victim...

On 5 February 2001, Armin saw a post from CATOR99, which read: 'I will offer myself up and will let you dine from my live body. Not butchery, dining!'

It looked like fate had delivered the victim Armin longed for.

Armin wrote back right away asking for more details.

CATOR99, whose real name was Bernd Juergen Brandes,

replied saying he was thirty-six years old, 175cm tall and weighed 72kg. He added that 'I hope you are really serious about it because I really want it.'

This looked like the real thing to Armin. 'There are a lot of people out there who are interested, but only a few who really mean it,' he wrote back as Franky.

'Whoever REALLY wants to do it, needs a REAL VICTIM!' came back Bernd.

Armin sent Bernd a photo of his teeth, saying: 'I will sink them into your body and bite off your tongue.'

'That won't be Hell, but Heaven on earth,' Bernd replied.

The bottom line was Brandes wanted to be castrated and eaten and Armin wanted to eat a young man. If it weren't so grotesque and strange it would have been a match made in heaven.

Arrangements were made for Brandes to visit Armin in Rotenburg on Friday, 9 March 2001. Both eagerly anticipated the meeting.

'I will reach my life's goal at last,' Armin told his willing victim.

Bernd replied, 'This is what I was born to do... I am your meat.'

Armin wasn't idle in the lead-up to the visit. He had to prepare the house for his guest. The first thing he needed to do was build a slaughter room. Bernd weighed between 100 and 200 pounds. Armin had read on cannibal websites that a 'long pig' of this weight could be manipulated by one person, but would need time and effort, not to mention space. He chose a room on the second floor of the farmhouse to create his makeshift slaughter room. He put hooks on the walls for hanging the carcass and constructed a trough for the blood to drain away.

He dragged a rusty old iron bed to the centre of the room and laid a blue floral mattress and quilt on top of the coiled metal springs. As a final touch he dropped some sturdy rope on the bed for restraining his victim.

An old metal patio table served as his butcher's slab – the holes in it would allow the blood to drain through to the concrete floor. He arranged various-sized sharp knives on the table, along with his late grandmother's axe.

Lastly, he soundproofed the room with old mattresses to mask any screams of pain.

Armin was proud of his work and duly posted photos of his slaughter room on the web, as well as emailing them to his list of cannibal contacts.

By this time, Armin was certain Bernd was genuine – that he wasn't a 'slaughterhouse tease' like Jörg had been.

Surprisingly, Bernd's background was relatively stable. There was little, if anything, to make you point your finger and say, '*That* must be what triggered his death wish.' He was born in 1958 to a middle-class family. His mother was an anaesthetist at a local hospital, his father a GP. So there was no question of an impoverished or deprived upbringing.

But in 1963, when Bernd was five, one of his mother's patients died as a result of a mistake she made. She couldn't forgive herself for the incident. So the family took a holiday in the hope it would help her overcome her feelings of guilt. Instead she was killed after driving into a tree.

With hindsight it would be easy to cite the death of

Bernd's mother as significant, and see it as the early catalyst for the death wish that led to him being cannibalised. While her death would undoubtedly have been traumatic, Bernd was hardly the first to have lost his mother at a young age. And not all children who lose their mothers grow up with a pathological self-destructive streak. What's more, when his father remarried three years later, Bernd got on very well with his stepmother.

He also did well at school and university, eventually qualifying in engineering with a good degree. This led to him securing a job at Siemens AG, Germany's biggest engineering firm. He tested software for telephone systems and became a world specialist in his field. After four years at the firm he was made head of department, and was considered popular by colleagues for being easy-going and fun to work with.

He had a long-term relationship with a woman called Ariane. She told friends he was a 'thinker, a good listener and an easygoing, domestic type. He's so stable and secure'. After seven years together they split up, having drifted apart. He then went out with a string of women. One relationship ended when he revealed, 'I have feelings for men – I'm bisexual.'

He eventually took up with a man – twenty-seven-year-old Rene Jasnik – whom he met at a party. They hit it off right away and Rene soon moved into Bernd's plush apartment. The two had a stable, loving relationship and had sex once or twice a week. Bernd never showed any sign of having a penchant for pain or torture.

But outside the relationship, it was a different matter. Brandes was secretly visiting male prostitutes that he picked up outside Bahnhof Zoo, Berlin's main railway station. He had started visiting prostitutes after splitting up with Ariane. By 1999 he sometimes went down to the station three times a day to live out his fantasies.

One prostitute – Immanuel, a fit Puerto Rican with tight curly hair and fashionable clothes – said Bernd started demanding increasingly violent sex, asking to be whipped until he bled.

'I only want you to stop torturing me when the pain becomes unbearable,' Brandes told Immanuel, later asking him to, 'Bite into my penis, bite it off!'

Immanuel played along not believing Brandes really wanted to be mutilated.

But then Bernd brought along a meat knife. 'Chop it off,' he said. 'You can do with it what you will.'

Immanuel refused.

In December 2000, Bernd offered another prostitute – Victor Enrique – 10,000 marks to bite off his penis. When he said no, Bernd threw his car and computer into the deal. This was too much for Victor. He felt he had no choice but to break off contact with Bernd, whose desires had turned far too weird.

It was around this time that Bernd turned to the web to find someone to fulfil his needs...

THE SLAUGHTER

Bernd's live-in lover Rene had a job at a bakery. As soon as he left for work, Bernd would log on to the web to surf cannibal websites and chat rooms. Under his screen name CATOR99 he'd post messages saying things like, 'Looking for a manly man to help me leave this world.' So when he saw one of Armin's adverts requesting 'people for slaughter' he didn't hesitate to reply.

'I've wanted to be slaughtered and eaten ever since I was a child,' Bernd told Armin, who said his cannibalistic desires had also begun in childhood.

Not surprisingly, they hit it off immediately and arranged to meet up on 9 March 2001, the plan being for Bernd to go to Rotenburg and meet his end in the slaughter room.

Both men looked forward to the meet-up with great anticipation. For them it would be a day of destiny; at last they would fulfil their life-long dreams.

When 9 March came, Bernd got up quietly so as not to disturb Rene. He had a shower and dressed in casual, but smart clothes. He erased his computer's hard disk so no one would have any idea where he had gone.

He'd made out his will a few days earlier, leaving the bulk of his estate, including his penthouse apartment, to Rene, who had no idea about his lover's strange, self-destructive desires.

Bernd paid for his train ticket in cash, again to avoid any possibility of being traced.

When he arrived at his destination, Armin was waiting to pick him up.

'I am Cator,' said Bernd. 'I am your flesh. I hope you'll find me tasty.'

Armin was relieved that Bernd hadn't pulled out at the last minute. He had been pretty certain Bernd genuinely wanted to be slaughtered; now he was almost totally convinced.

After driving back to the farmhouse, the two had coffee together and chatted, anticipating the blood-letting to come. They then got up and slowly peeled each other's clothes off. Armin said he'd wanted this for a long time but

wanted to be 100 per cent sure that Bernd really did want
to be slaughtered.

'Are you certain you want to go through with this?' he
asked. 'It's not too late to change your mind. I only want
someone who is completely willing to be eaten.'

'You have my word and my permission to kill me, if that
is what you need,' Bernd replied. 'I am your Cator, your
flesh, remember.'

Satisfied, Armin led Bernd to the slaughter room to show
off his grisly work. He also set up a video camera to record
the butchering that was to come.

Next, the two men made love together in a gentle, tender
way. This might sound odd considering their taste for pain,
torture and cannibalism. But it should be remembered that,
in their own peculiar way, they were soul mates; tragic
lovers on a par with Tristan and Isolde.

Once their tender embraces were over, it was time to up
the ante and explore the dark delights of pain.

Bernd said, 'I want you to bite off my penis so that you
draw blood. I want you to start to chew and bite the whole
thing off.'

Brandes was highly aroused by the thought that he was
about to experience his ultimate sexual kick. The only
problem was that Armin couldn't bring himself to carry out
Bernd's wish. Despite his extreme sexual fantasies, he didn't
want to hurt anyone.

'You're too nice, too weak,' said Bernd, a mixture of scorn
and disappointment showing in his voice. 'You're not tough
enough to carry it through. I should have realised earlier.'

He then asked Armin to drive him to the station so he
could catch a train home to Berlin.

Armin was devastated. His long-held dreams of killing and eating someone were about to be shattered – and it was all his own fault.

But mere words couldn't remedy the situation. Bernd wanted his penis bitten off and Armin simply couldn't bring himself to do it.

Resigned, Armin drove his disappointed lover to the railway station.

At the last moment, however – just before the next train to Berlin arrived – the two men decided it was worth a second try. Both agreed that Armin might find it easier if Bernd was semi-conscious for the castration. So they went to the station chemists for a packet of sleeping pills and a bottle of cold medicine, which Bernd slugged back, and then headed back to the farmhouse.

This time they didn't waste time with coffees. After Bernd had swallowed more sleeping pills and gulped back half a bottle of schnapps, the two went straight up to the slaughter room and lay down on the bed.

Bernd's head was beginning to spin when he said, 'Castrate me, Armin. Then kill me. Now.'

Recognising it would be too difficult to bite off Bernd's penis with his teeth, Armin decided to use a kitchen knife. Bernd was more than happy with this as it would leave a clean cut.

Armin switched on the video camera, while Bernd placed his erect penis on a breadboard, brought to the slaughter room by Armin for this very purpose.

Armin raised the knife high above his head and brought it down close to the base of Bernd's penis. Both men looked down … but Bernd's penis was still attached.

Armin tried again. Still the penis was intact. The knife clearly wasn't sharp enough.

Bernd was not about to give up now. 'Go and get a sharp knife,' he told Armin.

Armin dashed downstairs, found a sharp chopping knife, and charged frantically back upstairs. It was 6:30pm. At long last the bloodletting could begin.

Once more Armin raised the blade high in the air and brought it down on Bernd's still erect member. This time it had the desired effect. Bernd let out a blood-curdling scream of agony as he felt the blade cut into his penis. Armin had to bring the blade down twice more before Bernd's penis was fully severed from his body. Blood streamed down his thighs and his face was contorted with the pain. But he had no regrets. On the contrary, he felt elated. He was on an incredible high, having achieved what he most yearned for in life.

Although Bernd's aim was to die, he didn't want to bleed to death – not yet, anyway. He wanted a little longer to savour the torturous pain of his final hours on earth. So Armin bandaged his wound. He knew what he was doing as he'd learnt First Aid skills while in the army.

When Armin was done, Bernd said, 'How about an appetiser before your banquet, one that I can share?'

Bernd felt weak from the blood loss but was determined to see his gruesome fantasy through to the end. He wanted them both to eat his severed penis.

The two men rushed down to the kitchen, Armin clutching their macabre feast.

Armin cut it into two and arranged the pieces on a plate for them to eat. Unfortunately, being raw, the meat was too chewy and tough to swallow. Undeterred, Armin fried the pieces up with salt, pepper and garlic. This failed too. The slices of penis shrivelled up and turned black.

Although eating his own penis had been on his fantasy agenda, Bernd wasn't too worried. He was still ecstatic from being mutilated and was looking forward to his life slowly ebbing away.

The bleeding wound had made him cold and weak. All he wanted to do now was soak in a warm bath. So Armin helped him to the bathroom and ran him a bath. Seconds after he got in the water was running red with his blood.

Armin noticed that Bernd's face and lips were beginning to turn blue. But he seemed at peace and had a happy expression on his face.

'You've no idea how good this feels,' Bernd told him, his voice not much more than a whisper.

'I don't want anything to remain of me,' he added. 'I want you to grind up my skull and my teeth so there's absolutely nothing left. I want to be completely annihilated.'

Bernd's pulse was slowing down. Death was lurking in the shadows, ready to claim its unusual prize – a willing victim.

Armin asked him if he was okay. Bernd said he just wanted to sleep. So Armin heaved him out of the bath and put him to bed in the slaughter room.

Bernd had little life left, but he was still breathing. It was a waiting game now. So Armin went downstairs to read one of his Star Trek novels to kill time.

When he went back up stairs an hour or so later to check on Bernd, he had woken up.

Armin asked if there was anything he could do for him.

'Yes,' said Bernd. 'I want you to wait until I've lost

consciousness. Then I want you to slash my throat. I've lost so much blood, I don't think it will be much longer before I pass out.'

It was 3:30am when Bernd finally fell into unconsciousness. Armin pinched him and snapped his fingers close to his ear. He got no response. Bernd was out cold.

'Goodbye, my friend,' he said, kissing him tenderly on the forehead. 'It's time to say farewell.'

Armin clasped his hands together and said a prayer, asking God's forgiveness for what he was about to do. Then he reached for the chopping knife – the one he'd used to slice off Bernd's penis – and plunged it several times into his throat, killing him.

Bernd's death was neither dramatic, nor spectacular. He just pegged out as the blood gushed from his throat. But at least he had achieved his long-held desire to be slaughtered. And his death – although outlandish to most of us – was presumably a happy one.

My cannibal correspondent Eric Soames, however, didn't see Bernd's demise as happy; nor did he go along with the idea that he was a willing victim. As far as he was concerned Bernd's death was the inevitable result of demon possession. He believed Armin had been overtaken by a dark entity during his childhood. As it grew in strength this creature emitted a kind of magnetism that drew potential victims to Armin.

'I can't emphasise this enough, Bernd Juergen Brandes was not a willing victim,' he told me in one email. 'He was troubled and disturbed, but the demon that possessed Armin Meiwes had the power to draw people with fragmented minds and manipulate them into succumbing to the death impulse. It was able to override Bernd's survival instinct and make him literally lust for mutilation and death.'

Others see it differently. Shock rocker Marilyn Manson, for example, described the macabre relationship between the two men as a 'sick love' story and said it was the inspiration behind the title of his 2007 album *Eat Me, Drink Me*. In March that year Manson told *Revolver* magazine what the cannibal case meant to him. 'Although I can't relate to the relationship those two had,' he said, 'I found the story very compelling in a romantic way. I think a lot of people wouldn't look at it as romantic, but it was to them in a sick way, and it is to me in some sick way, too.'

FORBIDDEN FEAST

Now that Bernd was dead it was time for Armin to satisfy his lifelong craving to eat human flesh. At last he would get to taste 'long pork'. First, though, he had to see to the practicalities of preparing a freshly killed carcass to make it ready to eat.

He hung the corpse by its feet on a meat hook to let it bleed dry like you would a pig. Once this was done, Armin cut off the head and put it on a table so it could watch – and he could talk to it – as he disembowelled the body.

After gutting the carcass, he skinned it and sliced off the scrotum. He then cut off the arms and set about choosing the various prime cuts of meat, much as a high street butcher would do with an animal carcass. He lopped off sections of rump, upper leg, and thigh, then disposed of the offal and other waste.

'You'll soon become one with me,' he told the severed head.

Finally, Armin dug a grave and buried Bernd's bones, skin

and innards. During an impromptu funeral service he recited Psalm 23. 'The Lord is my shepherd; I shall not want,' he intoned solemnly. 'He maketh me lie down in green pastures; he leadeth me beside the still waters.'

Two days later Bernd's flesh was ready to be consumed. Armin was almost shaking with anticipation and excitement. But he didn't want to rush things. He wanted to make it a truly special occasion. So he laid the table with his late mother's best cutlery and plates, and decorated it with flowers.

Armin used a simple recipe to cook up a large steak from Bernd's flesh. 'I sauteed the steak of Bernd with salt, pepper, garlic and nutmeg. I had it with Princess croquettes, Brussels sprouts and a green pepper sauce,' he told German television in an interview from prison in October 2007.

Before tucking in he said grace:

Thank you for the world so sweet,
Thank you for the food we eat,
Thank you for the birds that sing
Thank you God for Everything, Amen.

He then added a verse in his own words:

Thank you for providing me with a friend for life
And for sacrificing Bernd's life on earth for me.
I hope I won't be lonely any more, Amen.

Armin picked up his knife and fork, cut a piece off the human steak and slowly, almost sensuously, placed it in his mouth. Although he found it a little tough, consuming human flesh was his epiphany, the culmination of everything he had dreamed of. The pleasure he felt was on a par with if he had spent decades saving himself for that special person, meeting them, and then having sex for the first time.

'The first bite was of course a peculiar, indefinable feeling at first because I had yearned for that for thirty years, that this inner connection would be made perfect through flesh,' Armin recalled later. 'The flesh tastes like pork, a little bit more bitter, stronger. It tastes quite good.'.

Armin firmly believed that by eating Bernd the two of them would be united forever. That their souls would somehow merge as one. He felt that he would no longer be lonely.

'In my imagination he is now also a part of me,' Armin said later. 'That is a good thought.'

Armin also felt that he had assimilated Bernd's skills, attributes and characteristics when he ingested his flesh. He felt stronger, more intelligent and more worldly-wise.

More curiously, Armin was sure Bernd had passed on his abilities at speaking English, a language Armin wanted to be fluent in, but hadn't exactly excelled in at school.

The following day it was time to try another dish. Armin decided to adapt pot roast for human meat. He sprinkled a nice tender cut from Bernd with salt and pepper and rubbed it in garlic. Then he lightly seared the joint in a pan and put it in the oven to roast for a few hours.

Over the next month or so Armin got through almost half of his victim, defrosting sections as and when he needed them. He'd eat bits of Bernd with his morning eggs, and even took slices of human meat to work with him to gulp down at lunchtime. For his evening meal he would cook up more lavish meals of human meat. He'd never enjoyed cooking in the past. Now he was a dab hand in the kitchen.

It would have been okay if it had ended there. Unfortunately his taste for human flesh hadn't been satiated with eating Bernd. He wanted more.

After Bernd failed to return home Rene, his lover, began to get worried. Maybe Bernd had found another guy? Was this the end of their relationship? Worries like this evaporated when he found the will Bernd had made out, leaving everything to him. Now he was wondering whether his lover had committed suicide. He just couldn't understand what was going on. He and Bernd had been such a stable couple.

In a panic Rene reported Bernd's disappearance to the police. They weren't overly concerned at first, presuming he had found another guy or just gone AWOL because the relationship was stifling him for some reason. This wasn't indifference on their part; the fact is, people do sometimes walk out on lovers without a word.

But when no word was heard from Bernd at all, the police began looking into the case. The only problem was their enquiries led nowhere. It was like the Marie Celeste. They couldn't find a single clue that might shed light on Bernd's whereabouts. It was as if he'd disappeared into thin air.

The police were stumped. There was little else they could do. It looked like Armin had got away with slaughtering Bernd, and would likely go to his grave with his grisly secret intact. No one had any inkling of the dark deeds that had gone on in his ramshackle farmhouse.

Deep down Armin was proud of what he'd done. To him, killing and eating Bernd was an achievement. After all, he'd accomplished his long-term aim in life. If you left out the murder and butchering aspects, he wasn't much different to Bill Gates or Steve Jobs, both of whom strived for success in the technology world and pulled off their ambitions. Naturally they are proud of their achievements. And rightly so.

It was the same for Armin. In his opinion he had done a good job, particularly when it came to preparing Bernd's carcass for eating. And the more he thought about it, the more he started to think he should do it again. Find another willing victim. After all, he was no longer a fantasist. He was as good as a professional when it came to killing and butchering human meat. So he logged back onto the cannibal internet forums as Franky.

He had high hopes that he would find another victim who wanted to be slaughtered. After all there were at least 1,800 active participants on cannibal forums such as Gourmet, Cannibal Cafe and Eaten Up.

So he placed another series of online adverts. One read: 'Looking for a well built, nice young man between eighteen and twenty-five for a real slaughter and feast. Please apply with statistics including age, height and weight. If possible with a photo.'

When he didn't get any takers he upped the age requirement to thirty. A number of men responded. But like the hotel cook Jörg from Villingen, Schwenningen, all turned out to be fantasists. They pulled out at the last minute when they realised Armin was for real. One guy looked very promising. He visited Armin, allowed himself to be chained up in the slaughter room and begged to be decapitated. It should have been a dream come true for Armin. But it wasn't. Armin was choosy about who he would slaughter. He considered the guy to be too stupid and too fat to be worthy of killing and butchering. While there is a certain irony in this, it should be remembered that Armin believed he would take on his victim's attributes after eating them. So it's understandable that he was picky about his victims.

Armin also turned down a guy who wanted his genitals burned with a flame thrower. He considered it way too weird.

SURRENDER

Up to now Armin had sensibly kept his activities to himself. But he wanted to tell people about what he'd done. He wanted the fantasists to know that he'd actually gone through with his dream of eating someone. He wanted to be crowned king of the online cannibals.

So he logged on to the cannibal chat rooms and boasted about how he'd killed and eaten a guy. It sounded very convincing. Most probably dismissed it all as imaginative, but not the real deal.

This is the way a university student from Innsbruck saw it. He'd got a taste for the bizarre and spotted Armin's postings on the web, which he thought were very vivid, but not for real. Nevertheless he was intrigued. So on 9 July 2001 he dropped an email to Franky offering himself up for slaughter. He was curious about what kind of reaction he would get.

Being keen, Franky wrote back promptly. The student's eyes went wide in horror as he read the email. It was way too convincing. 'This guy has really killed someone,' he whispered to himself in horror. Terrified and in a panic he deleted his Lycos email account so there was no chance of

Franky tracing him. After some thought he concluded that Franky was extremely dangerous, and went to the police. They took it seriously and followed it up. Two months later, after a good deal of detective work on cyber networks, they were able to ID Franky as Armin Meiwes.

The game was finally up.

Just before Christmas 2001 the German police swooped on Armin's farmhouse. It was 8:45am. They banged loudly on the door. Armin wondered who it could be. No one normally called this early. When he opened the door he knew his deadly deeds had come to light.

Sitting at the kitchen table the police asked Armin if he had killed and eaten a man as described on the cannibal forums.

Armin replied, 'I may have...'

Such an ambiguous answer was bound to raise suspicions. The detectives looked at each other, then immediately instigated a search of the farmhouse. They found unusual looking meat in the freezer. It could have been pork, but they were by no means certain. So it was sent off for tests.

The police then checked the hard drives on Armin's array of computers and found 3,842 hard-core porn pictures depicting torture scenes, mutilation and extreme violence. When the search moved upstairs they found the slaughter room with meat hooks on the walls and killing knives arranged neatly on the table.

As far as they were concerned they'd walked into the house of a psycho killer.

But they couldn't arrest Armin. They needed more evidence. At that point they could only have got him on a 'glorification of violence' charge.

After they'd left, Armin thought about his position. He

recognised there was no way out. It had been good while it lasted. But now he was going to have to face moral condemnation for breaking one of society's most deep-seated taboos.

So he decided to give himself up. But he wasn't stupid. He didn't go straight to the cops. He drove to a local lawyer, Harald Ermel, for informed advice on how best to proceed.

When he walked into the lawyer's office he said, 'I've done something stupid...'

Ermel thought Armin had probably been caught for speeding or drink driving. When Armin told him he'd killed and eaten someone, his mouth fell open. This wasn't the kind of thing he was used to. Once he'd drawn a breath and composed himself, he told Armin that he must give himself up. That way, things would go better for him in the long run.

Ermel called the cops on Armin's behalf and they promptly sent a squad car down to take him in.

Once in custody Armin told police, 'I admit what I've done. I accept that I'm guilty. And I regret my actions.' He then gave them Bernd's name so they could identity the victim.

Soon afterwards police were swarming through Armin's farmhouse. Sniffer dogs covered every inch of the house and grounds and a digger excavated the area looking for remains. They soon verified that Bernd had been Armin's only victim.

Armin fully cooperated. He showed police all the chat rooms and websites he'd been on, and gave them his usernames and passwords.

When police asked why he did it, Armin said, 'I got a kick

out of the idea of having another person inside of me. I had the fantasy and in the end I fulfilled it.'

Detective Wilfried Fehl was given the thankless task of evaluating the video recording of Bernd's slaughter and the dismembering of his body into meal-sized portions. He was utterly revolted. 'It's practically unimaginable what he did,' Fehl commented later.

With such graphic and detailed evidence, it should have been an open and shut case. The problem was that the video recordings – and the two men's email exchanges – revealed in no uncertain terms that Bernd really was a willing victim. And besides, Germany had no law against cannibalism.

Ermel insisted Armin should – at worst – be convicted of 'killing on demand', a charge with a maximum sentence of five years in prison and usually confined to cases of euthanasia. German authorities, however, filed murder charges against Armin and he was moved to a high-security prison to await trial.

Armin's trial began on 3 December 2003. Prosecuting lawyer Marcus Köhler told the court that Armin had made a video of the killing and butchering of Bernd so he could sexually satisfy himself later while watching it. Köhler had been forced to unearth a little-used legal statute – murder for sexual satisfaction – to make up for the lack of any law against cannibalism.

Armin took the stand – looking very smart in a tailored suit. He denied that this was the motive for the killing, then tried to explain why he had done it. He recalled how he had felt terribly lonely and neglected as a child after his father had walked out on the family, and how he had fantasised about having a 'blond youngest brother' who he could keep forever by 'consuming' him. He then said how he began thinking about cannibalism between the ages of eight and twelve, and imagined eating his school friends. Horror movies, he admitted, had heightened his desires.

He never once flinched when describing to the court the terrifying acts he had committed. He was very calm and matter-of-fact about the way he had slaughtered and cut up Bernd. It had become normality to him.

He was totally unrepentant. 'My friend enjoyed dying, death,' he told the court. Then added, with a smile towards the prosecution, 'Show me the statute that states that what I've done is against the law.'

He'd been studying law during his time in prison and knew that the prosecution were on shaky ground.

Unsurprisingly the story shocked the world. Mostly because Armin looked so ordinary. He could have been a bank manager. Yet he'd killed and eaten someone. He should have looked like a monster, but he didn't. It brought home to the world that even your next door neighbour could be a crazed cannibal killer. There was nothing to mark them out. Nothing to give them away. How could you know, until they wielded the knife? And then it would be too late...

Chillingly, when investigator Wilfried Fehl took the stand, he said that the gruesome case was not a one-off. His officers had discovered a flourishing cannibal scene in Germany. 'We are talking about dentists, teachers, cooks, government officials and handymen,' he told the horrified court.

Rudolf Egg, a criminologist in the German central criminal service, backed this up when he said there were several hundred people with cannibalistic tendencies in Germany alone, and many thousands more around the world. He pointed out, however, that unlike Armin, only a tiny proportion entering cannibal chat rooms were actually willing to carry out their fantasies for real.

But was Armin mad? Was he psychotic or deranged?

Not according to prison psychiatrist Heinrich Wilmer. He said that Armin was in good mental health but should be given psychotherapy. He believed Armin had a personality disorder and lacked 'empathy and self-control'.

Klaus Beier, a psychotherapist and sexologist at Berlin's Charite hospital, concurred. He said Armin couldn't be classified as mentally ill and shouldn't be sent to a mental hospital. Armin had 'at least average intelligence and showed no signs of psychiatric illness'.

A couple of other psychologists made reference to Armin's claims that he had been abused as a child by an older relative. He was allegedly forced to watch gay porn videos and encouraged to act out the scenes they portrayed.

On the twelfth day of the trial, prosecuting lawyer Köhler acknowledged that Bernd had been a willing victim; he had wanted to die at Armin's hands. But he added that Bernd may have been incapable of rational thought and Armin could well have taken advantage of this. On this basis he pushed for a life sentence, arguing that Armin was too dangerous ever to be released.

Armin's lawyer, Ermel, on the other hand, pressed for the lesser charge of killing on demand. 'My client is not a monster,' he said. He presented Armin as psychologically disturbed and claimed he had a sexual makeup that was fixated on human flesh. He went on to describe Armin as a 'gentleman of the old school', due to his good manners and politeness.

On the thirteenth day Armin said, 'Bernd came to me of his own free will to end his life,' adding that the only thing he personally regretted was he hadn't got to know him better before stabbing him.

Finally he stressed that he had satisfied his hunger for human flesh. 'I had my big kick and I don't need to do it again.'

The verdict was finally given on Friday, 30 January 2004. Judge Mütze convicted Armin of manslaughter and sentenced him to eight years and six months in prison, allowing time off for good behaviour. This meant he could walk free in four years and six months.

There was disbelief in court. Rene was appalled. This psychotic butcher and cannibal was being treated as if he were some sort of urbane 'gentleman' thief, like Raffles, and not a demented murderous monster. It seemed that justice was on the side of the criminal.

As part of his summing up, Judge Mütze did emphasise that what Armin had done was truly terrible and almost inhuman, but nevertheless was the result of two men with outlandish tastes coming together via modern technology which only ten years before hadn't even existed.

'The internet made this act possible,' he said. 'Two mentally disturbed people met each other there and reached an agreement. It was ethically and morally despicable. But both of them didn't care about that. They were two deeply psychologically disturbed people who both wanted something from the other.'

After the trial, the prosecution immediately launched an appeal. Prosecuting lawyer Köhler was adamant that Armin was a danger to society and should get a far more severe sentence.

In jail Armin became something of a celebrity. He got a lot of fan mail. He replied on the prison's old typewriter – a far cry from the computer equipment he was used to using. Predictably, he was inundated with requests for interviews from the media. But he was no fool. He knew his murderous act – however despicable it may have been – had made him bankable. So he declined all interviews unless the outlets were prepared to pay well for the privilege.

By this time he was thinking about his future career and how he could secure fame and fortune. As far as he was concerned he'd earned it. He'd done something that most people were not prepared to do. And, like it or not, that made him noteworthy in the eyes of the world.

His first proposed project was his autobiography. Publishers were already fighting for the rights to it. A movie was also on the cards. His lawyer, Ermel, believed it could net him a good million dollars. Although, out of that, he'd have to pay the court costs which amounted to around $140,000. But it would still set him up very nicely.

Armin had also become a big star on the cannibal scene. Websites were springing up everywhere in his honour. Some included adverts asking for willing victims.

Probably as a result of all the attention, Armin started to get above himself in prison. One Christmas, for example, he requested he be served a giant sausage for Xmas dinner – a Bockwurst banger. And he wanted it cooked in garlic and wine, the same recipe he had used to braise Bernd's body parts. Prison authorities were sickened by the request.

Armin's sentence was overturned in April 2005 and a retrial was ordered on the grounds that the lower court, in rejecting murder charges, had failed to give enough consideration to the alleged sexual motive behind the killing. It was the dogged persistence of Köhler that brought about the retrial. If it hadn't been for him, Armin would have got off lightly.

The retrial came just over a year later – in May 2006 – and Armin's sentence was increased to life imprisonment. Announcing the new verdict in a court in Frankfurt, presiding judge Klaus Drescher described the killing as a 'particularly perverse murder'. Armin was clearly disappointed. But he recognised that, given good behaviour and a positive assessment that he was no longer a threat to anyone, he could be out in fifteen years.

An expert on cannibalism, the writer Jacques Buval, however, is certain that Armin will never lose his hunger for human flesh. 'Cannibalism is a serial crime,' he told *The Times* newspaper during Armin's trial. 'If they let him free, he'll do it again. He won't be able to stop. They never can. It is in them like paedophilia. The Internet has created a fantasy universe for like-minded souls to connect. It may be just the tip of a vast iceberg that has been penetrated with this [case].'

Whether Armin will lose his taste for human flesh or not remains to be seen. But the world's most famous cannibal has certainly stopped eating animal meat. According to reports from winter 2007, Armin has converted to vegetarianism and was elected to lead the Green Party in prison. The group of Green supporters is made up of murderers, paedophiles and drug-dealers. They meet every Tuesday to discuss tax, legal and environmental policies.

Gerhard Kaehler, a Green Party representative working with the convicts, said, 'Armin is no fool. He can write and speak well. The group respects him; that is why he was voted as leader.'

Bavaria Radio reported a fellow inmate saying that Armin had vowed not to eat meat in his new role as environmentalist. 'He finds the idea of factory farming as distasteful as his crime was,' he said. 'He now sticks to vegetarian dishes.'

THREE:
NO MERCY

PETER BRYAN

It was hard to imagine how anything could top the horror of Armin Meiwes' cannibalistic feast. But then, just under three years later in early 2004, came the 'Kentucky Fried Human' case. The unsuspecting residents of Walthamstow, East London, could not have been prepared for the unspeakable horror that was about to be perpetrated on their doorsteps. It was as if the Devil himself had come to town (maybe he had) – such was the depravity of Peter Bryan's terrible act.

On 17 February the trusted care in the community patient left Newham General Hospital to visit his friend Brian Cherry in Walthamstow. Almost immediately the door was opened he launched a terrifying assault on forty-three-year-old Cherry, battering him to death with a hammer and then eating his brains with a knob of butter. When police later found him in Cherry's blood-splattered kitchen, he told them, 'I ate his brains; it was very nice.'

On the morning of that fateful day, doctors and careworkers at Bryan's mental health unit had agreed that the thirty-six-year-old could come and go as he pleased. Describing him as generally 'calm and jovial,' they had no concerns about his mental state and believed he was no threat to anyone. Yet by the evening he had killed and eaten his friend, and planned to kill others given t he chance.

Bryan met his victim through eighteen-year-old Nicola Newman who knew both men and lived locally. At 7:15 that evening she popped round to visit Cherry. She walked into a nightmare scene. The door was ajar. So she walked in. The first thing she noticed was a strong smell of disinfectant. Then she froze, riveted to the spot in terror. Peter Bryan was standing there, grinning insanely and brandishing a seven-inch knife. He was stripped to the waist and covered in blood. 'Brian is dead,' he said.

For a moment she didn't believe him – maybe it was some kind of sick joke? But then she noticed Cherry's body on the floor behind him. His right arm had been severed and was lying close by.

'Bryan went to shut the front door,' she later recalled, 'but I got there ahead of him and acted perfectly normal. I thought if I stayed any longer I might be the next victim. I just said, "See you later, Pete," and he smiled and shut the door after me.'

She then hurried to safety and called the police.

Although he turned into a crazed killer cannibal, Bryan's family background was fairly stable. His parents Frank and Jean came from Barbados. They joined the post-war exodus to Britain and settled in the East London suburb of Forest Gate. Frank, now in his early eighties, found work at the Ford car plant in Dagenham. Like many from the West Indies, they were a decent, God-fearing family. But there was one aspect of their lives they preferred not to speak about – the fact that a strain of mental illness ran through the family. Although his brother was also afflicted, it came out in Peter Bryan in a terrifying, deadly way.

After leaving school at sixteen Bryan found a job as a shop assistant in a fashionable boutique, in the Kings Road, Chelsea. Helping out alongside him in the evenings was the owner's daughter, twenty-year-old student Nisha Sheth. Bryan became infatuated with her, and would tease her and hide her possessions to gain her attention. But when he made advances towards her, she rejected them.

Not long afterwards – possibly in spite for being spurned – he returned to the shop while Nisha was in charge and stole some clothes. She reported this to her mother, Rahmid. When Rahmid confronted him, Bryan, who was now twenty-three, kicked her and hit her with a belt. Not surprisingly he was sacked on the spot.

Curiously, he hadn't got any previous convictions. But this incident proved the catalyst for him turning very ugly.

He was questioned by police about the assault, but nothing seemed to come of it. A week later, on 18 March 1993, Bryan left his home in Derby Street, Forest Gate, and went back to the shop. He was seeking revenge.

Nisha was on the phone in the shop, blissfully unaware of her impending fate. Her twelve-year-old brother, Bobby, was helping shut up shop for the night and was bringing in the display from outside. Bryan didn't hesitate. Armed with a claw hammer and high on cannabis, he struck Bobby twice over the head, knocking him to the floor.

The schoolboy managed to look up to see Bryan grab his sister and smash her five times over the head with the hammer. By the time the last blow was struck she was beyond saving and was dead before the ambulance arrived.

An hour later Bryan was in Battersea, South London. In an apparent suicide attempt, he climbed to the third floor of a building and hurled himself off. He survived. All that he injured was his feet.

The Sheths were obviously devastated at the death of their daughter. Whether intentionally or not, Bryan made their suffering even worse. While awaiting trial for killing Nisha, he sent a letter to her father. Displaying an appalling lack of sensitivity, he wrote:

> I am very, very, very sorry. I would have liked to be part of your family. But due to this situation this does not look possible. Telling to Nisha that I love her over and over again just does not work.

He then asked Nisha's father to send him some of her clothes:

> If you would be so kind to send me my clothes [he meant Nisha's] to HM Prison Brixton I would be very, very, very happy.

Lastly, with a chilling reference to his unrequited love for Nisha, he said:

> No one can tell me to keep away. Good luck.

• • •

Bryan's trial came in March 1994, a year after the killing. Diagnosed as a paranoid schizophrenic, he was convicted of manslaughter on the grounds of diminished responsibility and was sectioned in Rampton Hospital, Nottinghamshire, under the Mental Health Act.

His sentence stipulated he be held in the hospital's maximum security psychiatric unit 'without limit of time', which meant any eventual release would be down to doctors giving him a clean bill of mental health.

Bryan was very well-behaved in hospital. He came across as a charming, nice guy who didn't cause trouble. Because of his mental problems it started to look like he had been as much of a victim as Nisha Sheth; had it not been for his schizophrenia, it was reasoned, he wouldn't have killed anyone.

Nurses and social workers began to feel that the system had failed him and that hammering Nisha to death wasn't, strictly speaking, his fault. If only his mental problem had been diagnosed earlier Nisha might still be alive and he might be a free man – possibly working as an accountant, which had been one of his ambitions.

But it is all too easy to be taken in, to trust someone that comes across in an affable manner. If someone smiles warmly at us, for example, we generally smile back...

The fact was Bryan knew what he was doing. He was adept at hiding his mental problems and the strange, deranged desires that were growing in him.

He fooled everyone. By 2001 he was being granted regular leave from the hospital. In 2002 the Home Office was told he had made a full recovery. By the December of that year he was working as a cleaner, living in special accommodation, and was being lined up for a council flat.

But a month later there was a setback. He was accused of indecently assaulting a sixteen-year-old girl he had befriended. According to one account he 'blew raspberries' on her stomach. In any event, his behaviour scared her.

When a local lynch mob threatened to take revenge on Bryan, he was moved to Newham General Hospital in East London for his own protection. The alleged indecent assault probably should have set off alarm bells, but this didn't seem to be the case.

Numerous hospital and care home reports described him as stable and compliant. So in February 2003 he was moved to Riverside House, a residential care home in the Seven Sisters district of North London, and was given his own room key. However, while he was there he had a series of confrontations with staff. Despite this, reports still described him as presenting only a 'moderate risk of violence'.

On 17 February 2004 Bryan was taken to an open psychiatric ward at Newham General Hospital, where an hour-long review looked at his future. During the meeting, staff described him as 'calm and jovial' and it was agreed that he could become an 'informal patient'. This meant that Bryan would be able to come and go as he pleased from the hospital. It was one step away from living back in the community again.

As far as the staff at Newham General Hospital were concerned there were 'no concerns regarding his mental state and presentation'. He might once have battered someone's brains in with a hammer, but he now seemed like a relaxed kind of guy... yet by 7pm that very evening the brains of his next victim, Brian Cherry, would be sizzling in a frying pan.

Only hours after it was ruled he could come and go as he

pleased from Newham General Hospital, Bryan had bought a claw hammer and screwdriver from a building supplies store in Stratford – he wasn't planning on taking up DIY.

He then made his way to the Walthamstow council flat of his friend, forty-three-year-old Brian Cherry, who worked at Effjay shopfitters.

Cherry had also been treated for mental health problems. He was described as a 'nice man, lonely with no friends'. Unfortunately, the one friend he did make was bad news in the extreme.

As soon as Bryan got into the flat he began his murderous attack on Cherry, smashing the hammer twenty-four times into his head. He then scalped him and began chopping him up. He hacked off both arms and the left leg with a combination of a Stanley knife and various kitchen knives. Soon he was drenched in his victim's blood.

'I used the Stanley knife to cut them [the arms] off and some other kitchen knives, but I had to stamp on them to break the bone,' he related later.

Next he cut out Cherry's brain and fried it in butter.

The police were called at 7:40pm, having been alerted by Nicola Newman. On arrival they found Bryan standing in the hallway with blood dripping from his hands, jeans and trainers. Bloodstained knives were strewn around the floor, some of them smeared with fatty tissue. Brains – matted with hair and blood – were heaped on a plate, along with a knife and fork on the draining board. Nearby was an open tub of Clover butter.

Police later described the scene as being like a 'horror movie with blood dripping from the walls and limbs lying around in one of the rooms'.

Bryan told police he had killed Cherry after he opened the door, adding that he had enjoyed the 'forbidden fruit' of frying up and eating his victim's flesh and brains. He also revealed that the strips of flesh he ate from his victim's arms and a leg 'tasted like chicken'.

Chillingly – given the clean bill of mental health he'd just been given by Newham General Hospital – he told police, 'I would have done someone else if you hadn't come along. I wanted their souls.' He also admitted that the killing and cannibalism had given him a sexual buzz. As he killed Cherry, he said he fantasised about having sex with him alive and again after he was dead.

Finally the police had the unenviable job of bagging up the body parts and lumps of flesh, along with recording every spot of blood on the floor, walls and ceiling in Cherry's ground-floor flat.

In interviews with doctors and mental health experts Bryan claimed he killed Cherry as part of a Voodoo ritual to transfer the power of his victim to himself. Like the German cannibal Armin Meiwes, he wanted to absorb Cherry's attributes and characteristics. He believed that by eating the brain of a victim all the knowledge, feelings, anger and love they possessed would pass to him. This might sound like nothing more than the ravings of a madman. But dig deeper and you'll find that such notions – and practices – regularly occur in the world and, arguably, aren't necessarily perpetrated by the deranged.

The Democratic Republic of the Congo (formerly Zaire) in Africa, for example, is just one place that has been witness to terrifying, almost officially condoned cannibalism. The country was ravaged by thirty years of misrule under dictator Mobutu Sese Seko. After that it endured five years of anarchy and civil war in which around three million people died. Most were civilians, and most died as a result of the ensuing starvation and disease.

It was the worst calamity since World War II. But that wasn't the end of the horror. One of the rebel groups vying for power was the Movement for the Liberation of Congo (MLC). In late 2002 – partly under the leadership of a commander dubbed 'King of the Imbeciles' – the group launched a truly vicious offensive in the Ituri forest, in the wilds of the eastern Congo, which is home to tribes of Pygmies.

Towns were looted. Women and girls raped. Villagers were executed. And it was said that Pygmies were eaten.

Amuzati Nzoli, a Mbuti Pygmy, was widely quoted by the international press claiming that rebels attacked his jungle camp, cut up his family and grilled them over a campfire. They 'even sprinkled salt on the flesh they ate,' he said.

Sudi Alimasi, an official of the pro-government group Rally for Congolese Democrazy-ML, echoed these allegations. 'We hear reports of [enemy] commanders feeding on sexual organs of Pygmies, apparently believing this would give them strength,' he said. 'We also have reports of Pygmies being forced to feed on the cooked remains of their colleagues.'

A human rights worker with the 16,000-strong United Nations peacekeeping force in the Congo told *National Geographic* magazine in 2005 that: 'Cannibalism here is both an ancient tribal practice and a modern instrument of terror. But the attacks singling out Pygmies are new.

The prevailing theory holds that soldiers ate them to absorb their unique forest powers – good vision, tracking skills, whatever.'

This is exactly what Peter Bryan claimed to be doing – absorbing the 'powers' of Brian Cherry by eating him in some kind of Voodoo ritual. It could be argued that Bryan had seen reports in the newspapers concerning what might best be described as cannibalistic sorcery. Or possibly, due to his schizophrenia, certain aspects of his psyche, normally dormant, came to the fore. These might have contained memories of ancient magic involving eating people to gain power. Such memories may be contained in all of us, as all nations at one time or another have practised cannibalism. And even at its most benign – such as when far-flung tribes eat their dead relatives – cannibalism is still about soaking up power or attributes from the person being eaten.

The point is, Peter Bryan was not just deranged; in another culture his acts would have been perfectly acceptable. Had he been a member of the MLC and eaten a few Pygmies for their forest skills, for example, he'd have been given a pat on the back – certainly while the King of the Imbeciles was in power. They might even have appreciated his macabre wit too. When asked why he ate Cherry's brain, he came out with the ultimate one-liner: 'It was because the Kentucky Fried Chicken branch was closed at the time; it was definitely finger-licking good.'

The truly chilling aspect of the Peter Bryan case is that he could well have killed more people that night if he hadn't been disturbed by the visit of Nicola Newman. According to reports, he had already chosen another two victims because of his strong urges 'to taste the souls of men again'.

As it was he didn't get his chosen victims, but amazingly he did kill again.

After being charged with murder he was first remanded in Pentonville Prison, then moved to Belmarsh. There he assaulted two members of staff, and officers had to use shields when they entered his cell due to his 'unpredictable behaviour'. He was described as 'dancing around his cell like a boxer in training'.

Almost two months later – on 15 April 2004 – he was transferred to Broadmoor maximum security hospital in Berkshire under the Mental Health Act. Not before time, many thought. He spent three days in seclusion before being transferred to the Luton medium security ward with eighteen other patients. He was moved because he was thought to have 'settled'. Yet during this time he told one member of staff, who interviewed him, that he wanted to kill a warder and eat someone's nose.

Bryan had worked his magic yet again. He seemed to have the innate charisma of the fictional Hannibal Lecter; despite being a rabid, bloodthirsty killer he was able to work his charm on anyone.

He took full advantage of the small freedom he'd been granted. On 25 April, just seven days into his imprisonment at Broadmoor, he leapt on fellow inmate Richard Loudwell (fifty-nine) and smashed his head in. That day Loudwell – who was awaiting trial for the murder of an eighty-two-year-old woman – had been described as being 'happy, cheery and laughing'.

At around 6:10pm three members of staff heard two loud

bangs coming from the dining room, and found Loudwell lying on the floor next to a table and chair. His face was covered in blood and he had strangulation marks around his neck.

When Bryan was located he said, 'I smashed his head on the floor', and described how he had tried to strangle Loudwell. He added that, 'I would have eaten him too if I hadn't been interrupted.'

Loudwell died on 5 June from bronchopneumonia caused by severe brain injuries.

Bryan explained to doctors why he had attacked Loudwell. 'I get these urges, you see,' he said. 'I've had them ever since I saw him. He's the bottom of the food chain, old and haggard. He looked like he'd had his innings. I was just waiting for my chance to get at him. I wanted to kill him and eat him.'

When asked if eating people was normal, Bryan replied, 'Of course it's normal. Cannibalism is normal. It's been here for centuries. If I was on the street I'd go for someone bigger, you know, for the challenge. I wanted to cook him but there was no time nor was there access to cooking equipment. I briefly considered eating him raw.'

Bryan then named another patient as being next on his list to kill.

Bryan's trial was held in March 2005. Because of his unpredictability – and propensity for extreme violence – he had to be flanked by six burly guards. He pleaded guilty to two counts of manslaughter on the grounds of diminished responsibility. It looked like his terrifying game was finally up. Judge Giles Forrester gave him two life sentences, with no chance of release. In his summing up he said: 'The violence was extreme and unpredictable, accompanied by bizarre sexual and sadistic overtones. You killed because you got a thrill and a feeling of power when you ate flesh. You gained sexual pleasure from what you were doing.'

Bryan, of course, took all this with a pinch of salt (like he did when he ate Brian Cherry's brains). As far as he was concerned such behaviour was perfectly acceptable and he felt no remorse for it whatsoever. What's more, he was confident he would be able to charm his way out of life imprisonment and carry on his cannibalistic rampages. Shortly after commencing his sentence he was boasting that he could be free again in seven years. Now nicknamed 'Colonel Sanders' by fellow inmates – and merrily making 'finger-licking' gestures to other patients in Broadmoor – he said, 'If I play it right I'll be out in seven years, maybe less if I'm a good boy.'

Also during his summing-up, Judge Forrester made clear that the mental health services had a difficult job to do in deciding which inmates should be allowed to come and go as they pleased from secure care. In Bryan's case, he said, their job was made even harder: '[Bryan] had the ability to obscure the psychotic symptoms under a veneer of near-normality,' he stated.

That may be so. But the question is how many others are equally capable of duping the mental health services? Quite possibly more than we care to imagine. Michael Howlett, the director of the Zito Trust, an independent health watchdog, says, 'We estimate that between forty and fifty homicides are committed each year by those in contact with mental health services.'

How long will it be before another equally deranged killer like Bryan walks free to satisfy his deadly desires?

PAUL DURANT

2004 turned out to be a good year for British cannibals. In February of that year Paul Durant, an East Londoner on the run, was hiding out in Spain. During a row, Durant, who was also a heroin addict, reportedly killed his girlfriend, then chopped her up and ate her. In November 2007 he told a Spanish court how he had battered mother-of-two Karen Durrel to death with a mallet at her home on the Costa Blanca.

He was facing twelve years in jail after admitting manslaughter.

After his arrest Durant wrote to a newspaper claiming that he had butchered forty-one-year-old Durrel and eaten parts of her body after hearing voices in his head.

The forty-four-year-old wrote: 'After I killed her, I cut her body into small parts, eating what parts of her I found eatable. Before I killed Karen, I told her I had come to Spain where I was going to kill and eat paedophiles. I believed God had delivered her to me and I was getting messages from the telly. I believe she knew she had to die.'

Police searched the apartment the two shared and found blood in the bath and bloodstained knives, along with a saw.

But her body has not yet been found.

At the time of the killing, Durant was on the run from British police. He'd been arrested by the Flying Squad just before Christmas 2003. They'd caught him trying to snatch bags containing £38,000 from a guard outside a post office in Whitechapel, East London. There was a violent struggle during which a replica pistol was wrenched from his grasp.

Durant claimed he had been injured as police overpowered him and he was taken to the nearby Royal London Hospital for X-rays. Two policemen stood guard outside his ward. But he gave them the slip when he went for a cigarette.

Describing his escape, Durant said, 'I scaled the balcony. I escaped out of fear of going back to prison again. I have been in and out of institutions since the age of eleven.'

During the 1980s and 1990s he carried out a string of armed robberies on Post Office vans and security trucks netting around £500,000. Durant was also thought to have been involved in the drug trade and was the main suspect in the murder of a dealer in Stepney in the 1990s.

After escaping the hospital, Durant fled the country using a false passport. He then made his way to Spain in stolen cars and on buses and trains.

Karen, a divorcee from Ilford, Essex, had also decided to go to Spain. She and her boyfriend Miles Lanning, a builder, were in search of a better life. In January 2004 they settled in the village of Calpe, fifteen miles from Benidorm.

By February, Durant had arrived in Calpe and befriended them both. The three started drinking together and before long Durant had muscled in on Karen.

Lanning later said that the fugitive had not only stolen his girlfriend but threatened to kill him if he objected. He also said there was something strange about Durant:

I told her Durant was a weirdo loner and I warned her to steer clear of him but she seemed to feel sorry for him. He was grooming her. It was obvious he had his sights on her. He drove a wedge between us. We were short of money. I flew home to England to raise some more cash and as soon as I had gone he moved into our apartment. One evening there was a message on my answering machine from Durant. He said he thought I was a 'prick' for going back to England and if I came back he would kill me. But within a week he had killed her. I warned Karen about him. He had his sights set on her. He was on his own most of the time. He would just laugh to himself about nothing into thin air. It was a mad laugh. Her dad told me when we left for Spain, 'Look after my daughter.' Now I feel like I let him down. I carried her suitcase from the airport. The idea that he chopped her up and put her in that suitcase, it's all I can think about.

Durant battered Karen to death with a mallet after an argument about a video. 'They were watching a film in which children were sexually abused when they started to argue about its contents,' said a spokesperson for the prosecution. 'In the course of the argument, the accused left the room and returned with a mallet, which he used to hit her about the head from behind, provoking her death. Paul took the body to the bathroom and put it in the bath, where, using a knife and a saw, he cut it up and put the different parts of the body into plastic bags. The mutilated body was taken away, unknowingly, by rubbish collectors.'

Spanish police spent weeks searching the rubbish bins in the area, but couldn't find any trace of Durrel's body. Her pet terrier Louis, which she bought for £500 when she arrived in Spain, hasn't been found either. Police believe it suffered the same fate as its owner.

When Durant was arrested he told officers, 'I have committed many more crimes.' He even claimed he had told police in Britain of his cannibal tendencies on numerous occasions during his three decade-long criminal career. 'I had a previous desire to kill and eat people and told the British police so when I was held in the past,' he said.

When Durant's story hit the headlines, his former landlady Natalie Sanchez, revealed how he had terrorised her just days after he killed and ate Karen. 'He was constantly phoning and trying to hunt me down,' she said. 'He had an evil stare and now I think that it could have been me who was killed.'

Durant had lived in Natalie's apartments in Calpe before moving in with Karen.

'I was sorry for him," she said, adding that he soon started to make her feel uneasy. 'He'd start crying, then break into laughter. One time I gave him a hug but he started crushing me and I couldn't breathe. He was a complete madman.'

ROBERT PICKTON

One of the most chilling cases of serial murder the world has seen in recent times involves Robert 'Willie' Pickton, the notorious pig farmer from British Columbia in Canada. Although he didn't have any particular penchant for cannibalism, he allegedly included human meat in the sausages he sold.

During his trial in 2007, fifty-seven-year-old Willie – whose father was born in England – sat in a booth of bulletproof glass staring blankly as ex-friends revealed how he reportedly butchered and mutilated women. So gruesome were the testimonies and evidence that news accounts carried warning labels for graphic content.

Five years after his arrest in February 2002 he was on trial for six of the twenty-six murders he was charged with. The other twenty killings will be dealt with in a second trial some time in 2008. The true number of Willie's victims, however, is believed to be much higher than twenty-six.

As the end of 2007 approached, an estimated $100 million had been spent on the Pickton case, the largest investigation in Canadian history.

Police dug for bones at Willie's run-down suburban property for eighteen months after cops pulled him in. They unearthed the remains or DNA traces of dozens of women, all drug-addicted prostitutes, most of them picked up from the red-light district of Vancouver. But that could just be the tip of the iceberg, as police are still investigating the disappearances of dozens of other women.

The Downtown Eastside area where Willie picked up his victims is a stricken wasteland. Underage prostitutes walk the 'Kiddie Stroll' while addicts openly puke and writhe in agony on the pavement.

According to statistics, which haven't changed for years, about half of the 15,000 residents in the areas are drug users; about 90 per cent of them have hepatitis C; and about 30 per cent have HIV/AIDS, the same rate as Botswana.

No wonder United Nations officials described it as one of the world's worst slums in an affluent city.

In February 2002, days after his arrest, Pickton was in good spirits, laughing and joking with a cellmate. He said his murder spree was 'bigger than the one in the States'. He was referring to the Green River killer, Gary L. Ridgway, who was convicted of forty-eight murders. Pickton told his cellmate he had topped this and killed forty-nine women. 'I was gonna do one more, make it an even fifty,' he said, '[but] I make my own grave by being sloppy.'

Unbeknown to Willie his 'cellmate' was an undercover police officer planted by investigators, and every word of the conversation was recorded and later played back to the jury at his trial.

Willie, however, laughed when told he was suspected of being Canada's worst serial killer.

A video of his first interview with police shows him repeatedly chuckling and shaking his head. 'I'm just a pig man,' he told one of the officers. 'That's all I have got to say. Asked how he felt about being suspected of the murders of more than fifty women, he replied, 'What it means to me? Hogwash. I'm being set up.'

In the courtroom in New Westminster observers noticed something odd about Willie. He never once fidgeted in his seat. He didn't even rub his nose or scratch his eyes from time to time. His stillness was almost yogic, like he was a fakir of sadistic murder. Neither did he show emotion. He just sat still with his head slightly tilted. He didn't even look from side to side; nor did he turn his head to glance back to where relatives of some of the women he was accused of killing sat following the proceedings. Some of them, on the other hand, had to leave the room to get their emotions under control after hearing some of the gruesome testimony.

At the early preliminary hearings, when the court had to decide whether there was enough evidence for Pickton to stand trial, he wrote a lot on a pad of paper. Reporters wondered what he was writing. It's still not known.

• • •

Willie has often been described as slow-witted and foul-smelling, with unkempt stringy hair and a receding chin. This may well be the case. But he is also relatively wealthy. When he went cruising for prostitutes his pockets were stuffed with the profits of his family's land sales to housing developers in the Vancouver suburb of Port Coquitlam.

It was on one of the remaining sections of his family's land – seventeen acres, co-owned with his brother and sister, which included Willie's pig slaughterhouse – that police found the remains of butchered women.

Three severed heads and various hands and feet were found in buckets, while jawbones were buried among pig manure. A number of packages of meat were found to be contaminated by human DNA.

In July, a one-time friend testified that Willie had once described how he handcuffed and strangled prostitutes, then butchered the bodies and fed them to the pigs. 'You wouldn't believe how much blood comes out of them,' Pickton allegedly told the man.

What was left of the victims after the pigs had their fill went to a rendering plant. Chillingly, it is quite possible that people in the area became inadvertent cannibals. When the case first came to light, health officials issued a 'tainted meat advisory' to neighbours who might have bought pork from his farm, concerned the meat might have contained human remains.

The prosecution's key witness, Lynn Ellingsen, testified that she once walked in on a blood-covered Willie as he was gutting a woman's body hanging from a chain in the slaughterhouse. She said Willie told her that if she said anything she'd 'be right beside her'.

Another witness – Andrew Bellwood, who had lived briefly on the farm – testified that Willie told him how he strangled his victims while he had sex with them in his trailer – making him a necrophiliac the moment their life ebbed away. Andrew Bellwood also said Pickton told him he would take the bodies out to his slaughterhouse where he would gut and butcher them.

If all the allegations were true, the begging question is how he got away with it for so long. Pickton wasn't exactly a loner. A lot of people came and went on the farm. And regular, riotous parties were held there too. The first murder Willie is charged with occurred in 1995. And for seven years before Pickton's 2002 arrest, his brother, Dave, lived on the property. A troop of underworld characters, including women who worked as madams for Pickton, procuring prostitutes on the Downtown Eastside, were also frequent guests.

You'd have thought his game would have been up before it started. But it wasn't.

Mary Lynn Young, a journalism professor at the University of British Columbia, says, 'We don't know how [so many] women could go missing over twenty years in a city like Vancouver [without someone suspecting something]... We need to understand how it could happen.'

Larry Campbell, a former Mountie and mayor of Vancouver from 2002 to 2005, believes it was simply down to the fact that the police didn't have much to work with. 'You've got no crime scene, no body, and how many suspects out there? You're starting with nothing. And many times in those cases, people went missing and were [only] reported missing years later.'

But as far as Willie is concerned he had nothing to do with it. He insists he is just a 'plain little farm boy' who has been 'nailed to the cross'.

This didn't wash with the jury, however. On 9 December 2007, Willie was found guilty on six counts of second degree murder and was sentenced to life in prison with no eligibility for parole for twenty-five years. His ultimate fate won't be known until the second part of his trial concludes, which could be a year or more away.

DANIEL RAKOWITZ

In summer 2000 Daniel Rakowitz was on Court TV in the US recalling how he killed and ate his girlfriend just over a decade previously. He sat in the corner of his grimy cell, laughing one moment, squashing a mosquito the next.

He pulled out a copy of *Mein Kampf* and mumbled something about Hitler and Satanic numerology. Then, his face totally impassive, he related how he killed twenty-six-year-old dancer, Monika Beerle, and dismembered her body.

'I punched her one time and hit her in the throat. She wasn't moving no more after that. I thought she might be holding her breath so I went out to make a [marijuana] delivery,' he said. 'I came back two hours later and she was cold. Then I went ahead and did what I did. I dissected her totally. I just started chopping her up and cooking her meat.'

Rakowitz was a well-known character around Tompkins Square Park in the East Village area of Manhattan, New York, in the late 1980s. He hung out with the punk/alternative crowd that squatted in the park. But he was considered an oddball even amongst this radical group.

Apart from dealing marijuana, he worked as a short-order

cook and was often seen walking around with a chicken on his shoulder, mumbling about the Devil and police control. He also regularly declared that he was Jesus and would be taking over the country – his first act in power being to legalise marijuana.

Most people saw him as a harmless nut. Until 19 August 1989, that is, when the news broke that he had murdered and eaten his girlfriend, Swiss student and dancer Monika Beerle, with whom he shared an apartment on 700 East 9th Street.

The twenty-six-year-old, who was studying at the Martha Graham School of Contemporary Dance, only moved in with Rakowitz because she was in desperate need of an apartment. She lived with him for sixteen days before Rakowitz launched his deadly attack on her. He then spent the next few weeks dissecting her and boiling her remains on the kitchen stove.

One friend actually walked in while Beerle's head was in a pot on the stove, but didn't alert the police. 'I didn't want to hurt him anymore,' the young woman explained, suggesting she might have been one string short of a Fender Stratocaster.

When he was done Rakowitz put what remained of Beerle – her skull and bones – in a five-gallon bucket which he deposited in a locker at the Port Authority bus station.

Rakowitz then hit Tompkins Square Park to brag to his squatter friends about the killing. But no one believed him. He'd clearly got bored of his Jesus line, and now was going for something more macabre to get attention.

Still he'd made them some nice soup, which he ladled out to them. Unbeknown to them at the time the 'tasty' concoction was made from Monika's meat...

Michael, now in his late thirties and a psychologist, is a former punk who used to hang out in Tompkins Square Park in the 1980s with a group that included Rakowitz. He declined to give his full name but said he personally didn't drink the soup, although he knew some homeless people who had tasted it. Unsurprisingly they wanted to kill Rakowitz after finding out what they'd eaten, and how they'd become inadvertent cannibals.

'When I think about [Rakowitz], I kind of associate him with the nihilist crowd,' says Michael. 'I remember him wearing button-up shirts, kind of plaidy. I remember he used to dress more on the beatnik style. He had long, blonde hair and a beard. He wasn't into the punk scene, so he stood out.'

Police eventually got wind that a grisly homicide had been committed by Rakowitz and picked him up. He gave them a bizarre and disjointed confession laced with talk of Satanism, animal sacrifice and the new 'religion' that he had founded.

In a later interview with police he said, 'I'm the new Lord, and I will take the leadership of the Satanic cultists to make sure they do everything that has to be done to destroy all those people who do disagree with my church. And I'm going to be the youngest person elected to the US presidency.'

Born in 1960 in Rockport, Texas, Rakowitz had shown signs of mental illness early on, and had been given psychiatric care and medication. He moved to New York around 1985 and drifted into the alternative punk crowd who tolerated his eccentric nature.

Rakowitz was found not guilty of Monika's murder by

reason of insanity on 22 February 1991 and was incarcerated in a state hospital for the criminally insane.

He made an abortive parole attempt in 1995, then tried again in summer 2004, but was rejected after the jury were told that he still threatens to kill and eat staff and inmates at Kirby Forensic Psychiatric Center on Wards Island, where he is being held.

JOEY CALA

In 2001, in Fort Worth, Texas, ex-convict Joseph Frank 'Joey' Cala was another who suddenly burst into the news as a cannibal. The forty-one-year-old beat his seventy-nine-year-old mother to death, then cut her open and ate some of her heart. Police found Cala standing over his mother Lydia's body, blood dripping from his mouth.

When they took him into custody he said he worshipped the Devil and that they had interrupted his 'sacrifice'.

A medical examiner testified that Cala had bludgeoned his mother to death with his fists or feet, then cut open her chest and abdomen before removing some of her organs.

Cala had been living with her since he was paroled from a drink driving conviction in December 2000. He had also served time for drug possession and aggravated assault of a public servant. Dr Kelly Goodness, a forensic psychologist, said Cala appeared to suffer from schizophrenia and had been on medication for the condition.

Cala pleaded guilty to murdering his mother and was sentenced to thirty years in prison, but will be eligible for parole in fifteen years.

Cala's sister, Lydia Loggins, said her family were still not healed, despite the long sentence handed out to her brother.

'He has ruined our family,' she said. 'As far as I'm concerned, he should never get out of jail. I still love him, but it will take a long time to forgive.'

Lydia last talked to her mother on 14 October 2001 on the phone. Neighbours reported seeing the diminutive old lady working in her rock garden on the morning of 15 October. Police were called to check on her that evening when she failed to answer the phone. 'I looked through a window and saw him [Joey Cala] standing naked in a bedroom,' said Kevin Meador, one of the first officers on the scene. 'He was looking up, and it appeared that he was having a conversation with someone, but no one else was in the house.'

Police found Lydia Cala's body in the bedroom where Joey Cala had been standing. Presumably he'd been talking to the diabolic entities inside his head... an all too common scenario with killer cannibals and a thread we will analyse in some depth later on.

FOUR:
A TERRIBLE
ARTISTRY

ISSEI SAGAWA

It was nearly midnight on 13 June 1981. A middle-aged couple were enjoying a late night stroll in Bois de Boulogne, a large park in Paris, when they noticed a blue Peugeot 504 taxi pull up a short distance ahead of them.

A slightly built young man got out, paid the driver, and heaved two suitcases out of the taxi. After it had driven off he started dragging the cases towards the largest of the park's lakes. Just then he looked up, saw them staring, and panicked – quickly dumping the cases under a bush and running off into the night.

Curious, the couple walked over to look at the suitcases, wondering what he was so keen to dispose of. A bloody hand protruded from one of the cases, making them recoil in horror. They then hurried off to call the police.

When investigators arrived they opened the first case and

found the limbless, headless torso of a young woman. Packed into the other one were her arms, legs and head.

The suitcases and their grisly contents were taken to the mortuary, where an autopsy established that the body was that of a young woman who had been killed by a single gunshot wound to the back of the neck. Further inspection of the corpse revealed that some parts of the body were missing: chillingly, a knife had been used to slice off the tip of her nose and to cut pieces of flesh from her buttocks and thighs.

One thing in particular about the find puzzled investigators; the purpose of the dismemberment seemed only to be to make the body fit into the cases. Most murderers would mutilate the body to make it hard to identify. Yet the young woman's head and hands were almost intact, save for the bits that had been sliced off.

From the couple's description the police knew they were looking for a small man of Oriental appearance. The only problem was that a cosmopolitan city like Paris was full of such men.

The only clue they had to work with was that the suspect arrived at the Bois de Boulogne by taxi. So detectives began the long task of contacting every taxi firm in the city to see if one of their drivers recalled picking up an Oriental man with two unusually heavy suitcases.

Their luck was in. Forty-eight hours later a cabby said he not only remembered the guy, but could even point out the building where he had picked him up.

Just two days after the discovery of the dismembered body, six heavily-armed police officers burst into an apartment building on Rue Erlanger in Paris's fashionable

Auteuil district. They climbed warily up to a second-floor studio flat that had been let to Japanese student Issei Sagawa. He was the only man in the building who fitted the description given by the two witnesses.

With weapons ready – fearing they were about to be confronted by a monster – they rang the bell. To their surprise (and no doubt relief), the man who opened the door was a diminutive and quietly spoken thirty-two-year-old.

Sagawa, who was very cooperative, told them he had come from his native Japan to study at the Sorbonne School of Oriental Studies in Paris. He then openly confessed to the murder, claiming he had a history of mental illness.

A look in his fridge quickly brought them to the conclusion that 'certifiably insane' might have been a better description. On the shelves was a woman's breast, a lip and two buttocks, which he admitted slicing from his victim. Sagawa said he had eaten the missing parts from the body 'sliced thin and raw'. The experience, he said, was as satisfying as he had always imagined it would be.

Sagawa agreed to go to the police station without protest. When interrogation began he spoke matter-of-factly about the events of 13 June. He admitted calling a taxi and taking the two heavy suitcases filled with a human torso and body parts to Bois de Boulogne with the intention of disposing of them in the lake.

Then, in a quiet, almost apologetic tone, he told police how he had killed the girl and cut her body into pieces in the bathroom of his apartment.

The corpse hadn't yet been identified. But Sagawa – ever obliging – named her as twenty-five-year-old fellow student Renée Hartevelt, from the Netherlands. She had been a beautiful blonde intellectual who spoke three languages, and was in Paris studying for her PhD in French literature at the Censier Institute. She funded her studies by teaching languages and came across Sagawa when he asked her to teach him German. He told her he could pay her handsomely. Unlike Renée, he didn't need a part-time job to support his studies – he was the son of a wealthy and influential Tokyo businessman.

Sagawa was also an intellectual (he had a genius-level IQ), and had been an avid reader from an early age, as well as appreciating Impressionist paintings from the age of five. He'd already got an MA in Shakespeare studies and was now working for his doctorate in comparative literature.

Because she needed the money, Renée agreed to teach Sagawa German. And besides, she rather liked him. They had a lot in common and soon became friends. They talked about literature and went to concerts and dances together. He wrote her love letters, but she wasn't interested in him in a romantic way.

When they danced together Sagawa would imagine her nude body with its 'white flesh'. Any red-blooded male would do the same. But unbeknown to Renée his appetites were not just sexual. In an interview with Britain's *Observer* newspaper in 1992, he said, 'I admire very much beautiful girls, especially Occidental girls who are healthy and tall. On the other hand, I also have this aspiration, this strange desire for cannibalism.'

He blamed this penchant on a childhood nightmare in which he and his brother were being boiled in a pot. 'It was my first nightmare of cannibalism... not to eat someone, but to be eaten'. When he reached fifteen the tables had turned and he was regularly fantasising about eating human flesh.

It was only a matter of time before he got the urge to act out his desires. While studying for his degree in English literature at Wako University in Tokyo he made an abortive attack on a woman from Germany who, like Renée, was teaching him German.

'In my head there was always a fantasy of cannibalism, and when I met this German lady in the street, I wondered if I could eat her,' he told *The Observer*. So one summer's afternoon he climbed through the window of her ground-floor apartment. 'She was sleeping and almost naked. I wanted to attack her with an umbrella but I was a little scared, and when I got close to her, she woke and screamed. She was stronger than me. I fell down, and tried to escape. I couldn't tell people it was because of cannibalism. I was too ashamed.'

The incident occurred in the late 1970s. After this Sagawa went to Paris to study. One of the first things he did on arrival was buy a .22 rifle. He later told police he'd heard there were a lot of murders in the city and needed it for protection.

But he was also looking to satisfy his hunger for human flesh and made a number of abortive attempts at shooting local prostitutes he had picked up and taken back to his room. '[When] I have them in my house, in my room,' he related later, 'I tried to shoot them but I couldn't, really couldn't. It's not the sense of morality or something. I don't think so. I was scared.'

But then he met Renée. She had no suspicion of the dark desires that lurked within him. She wrote to her parents telling them about her new friend, describing him as 'a brilliant Japanese student'. She invited him to her apartment to discuss literature and take tea with her. She teased him about his less than adequate command of French, saying that she would have to teach him French as well as German.

In turn Sagawa invited her to his apartment to continue their discussion of literature. She willingly accepted. He served tea liberally laced with whisky, then brought the conversation around to his feelings for her. He told her he loved her and wanted to have sex with her.

Embarrassed, Renée said she really liked him, but her feelings were purely platonic. Sagawa nodded and said he understood. To dispel the awkward moment, he reached for a book of Expressionist poetry by the German poet Schiller and asked Renée to read it aloud.

He recounted what happened next in his semi-fictional autobiography *In the Fog* (1983), which was written during his incarceration in a French mental hospital (and he's described the murder to the media countless times):

She starts to read. She speaks in perfect German. I reach for the rifle hidden beside the chest of drawers. I stand slowly and aim the rifle at the back of her head. I cannot stop myself.

I aim and I fire. There is a loud sound and her body falls from the chair on to the floor. It is like she is watching me. I see her cheeks, her eyes, her nose and mouth, the blood pouring from her head. Too much blood, her face all completely pale. I try to talk to her, but she no longer answers.

He then undressed her, revealing her 'beautiful white body'.

I touch her ass. It is so very smooth. I wonder where I should bite first. I decide to bite the top of her butt. My nose is covered with her cold white skin. I try to bite down hard, but I can't. I get a knife from the kitchen and stab it deeply into her skin.

Suddenly a lot of sallow fat oozes from the wound. It continues to ooze. Finally I find the red meat under the sallow fat. I scoop it out and put it in my mouth. I chew. It has no smell and no taste. It melts in my mouth like a perfect piece of raw tuna in a sushi restaurant. I look in her eyes and say: 'You are delicious.'

He then spread Renée's lifeless legs and had sex with her corpse, telling her he loved her as he stroked and caressed her dead flesh. In one fell swoop, Sagawa had broken two taboos: eating human flesh and copulating with the dead. The small inoffensive student with a lisp had become a monster worthy of the terrifying Old Ones from the horror stories of H.P. Lovecraft, who saw humans as little more than a convenient hors d'oeuvre.

In fact, some esotericists believe that Lovecraft was unconsciously writing about real evil forces that occasionally surface in our world – usually through a human agent that they have possessed. This was very much the opinion of my cannibal informant Eric Soames. When you consider Sagawa's actions it is hard to see him as human. Indeed Soames insisted that Sagawa displayed numerous indications that an ancient, evil force was operating through him. 'He had an uncanny ability to come across as benign,' he said. 'That's the power of the entity, mesmerising law enforcement officers and others – and bear in mind Sagawa was the cannibal who went free and became a celebrity. His books like *In the Fog* spread an unholy and truly sickening message of the joys of eating human flesh. Make no mistake, Sagawa was and is possessed by a force whose baleful power reaches back through eternity.'

Although Soames himself had a strange and terrible desire to eat human flesh – and believed he also was possessed – he fought it with all his might. Arguably Sagawa had no human will left and thus relished his acts and felt no remorse. Soames, on the other hand, literally detested himself. Which was why he had come to me for help. But it was only as we came towards the end of our cyberspace exchanges that I came up with an idea that might help him and free him from his curse. Whether what I did for Soames – which he claimed 'saved his soul' and is related at the end of his book – would have had any effect on Sagawa is debatable. As Soames said during one of our talks, 'Sagawa was too far gone for anything to be done, he had no humanity left.'

Once Sagawa reached orgasm and deposited his semen inside Renée's lifeless, decaying vagina, he decided he was hungry again and, as recalled in his fictionalised autobiography, *In the Fog*, he ate some more of her flesh.

Finally I cut off her private parts. When I touch the pubic hair it has a very bad smell. I bite her clit, but it won't come off, it just stretches. So I throw it in the frying pan and pop it in my mouth. I chew very carefully and swallow it. It is so sweet. After I swallow it, I feel her in my body and get hot. I turn the body over and open her buttocks, revealing her anus. I scoop it out with my knife and try to put it in my mouth. It smells too much. I put it in the frying pan and throw it in my mouth. It still smells. I spit it out.

After that Sagawa used an electric carving knife to cut up Renée's body. He carefully sliced off sections of flesh to store in the fridge to eat later. He then became sexually aroused again.

Her hand still wears a ring and a bracelet. When I see her long fingers I am driven by another impulse. I use her hand to masturbate. Her long fingers excite me.

It was then he noticed her nose.

She has a small nose and a sweet lower lip. When she was alive I wanted to bite them. Now I can satisfy that desire. It's so easy to bite off her nose. As I chew the cartilage I can hear the noise. I use a knife to cut off more of the cartilage and put it in my mouth. It really doesn't taste very good. I scoop out her lower lip with my knife and put it in my mouth. It has hard skin. I decide to eat it later when I can fry it. So I put it in the refrigerator.

In between his butchering, Sagawa took photographs of his handiwork. He also took time off to go and watch a movie with friends. After a supper of raw flesh, Sagawa went to bed. He needed a good night's rest for the busy day ahead.

The next morning he went out and bought a luggage trolley and two large suitcases, along with a carpet cleaner.

He put what was left of Renée in black plastic bin bags and put them into the suitcases. He then called a taxi and tried to find somewhere suitable to dump the body parts. He failed miserably. In total he made three attempts to get rid of Renée's body, but there were always too many people about.

It was four days after the murder that he took the blue taxi down to Bois de Boulogne and made his abortive attempt of dumping the suitcases in the lake. It was no surprise he was spotted. The sight of this tiny Oriental man heaving two suitcases, which dwarfed him, across the vast expanse of lawn was bound to draw attention.

Maybe he didn't care? Maybe he believed he could get away with anything?

Sagawa seemed to think so. While awaiting his trial he was quoted as saying, 'I know now what to do when killing a girl, how not to be arrested.'

Empty words? It seems not. In 1983 a judge ruled that Sagawa was not mentally fit enough to stand trial, and that all criminal charges would be dropped because he was in a 'state of dementia' at the time of the murder. Instead, he decreed that Sagawa should be incarcerated indefinitely in the Paul Guiraud Hospital, a secure mental establishment in the Paris suburbs. After assessing him, hospital psychiatrists said he was an untreatable psychotic.

That should have been the end of that. But it wasn't. Not long after entering the Paul Guiraud hospital, Sagawa found he had become a star. A Japanese film company approached him about turning his life story into a movie. Then, celebrated Japanese playwright Juro Kara began exchanging letters with him. In 1983 these were published in the form of a novel called *Letters from Sagawa*. The book became a bestseller and won a literary prize for its 'interesting approach'. The Rolling Stones chronicled the case in their song *Too Much Blood* from the 1983 *Undercover* album. Meanwhile Sagawa was writing the first of a string of books, *In the Fog*, which, as we've already seen, included graphic descriptions of the killing and dismemberment of Renée. It became an overnight success in Japan, with the newspaper *Tokyo Shimbun* declaring it as 'beautifully done, and outstanding among recent Japanese literature, which has become boring'.

Within a year of his hospitalisation, Sagawa was released from the Paul Guiraud hospital and taken back to Tokyo. By the 'agreement of his parents' he was admitted to the Matsuzawa Hospital rather than being officially committed. Fifteen months later, in 1985, Sagawa's father decided it was time his son left the hospital. Unable to object, they let him out.

He now lives in a third-floor apartment in a suburb of Tokyo. His walls are hung with his own paintings, which depict Western women and highlight their fleshy pink buttocks.

He is totally unsupervised, despite the fact that Dr Tsuguo Kaneko, the superintendent of the Japanese hospital where Sagawa stayed before his release, believes he is a dangerous psychopath who should be prosecuted for his crime. 'I think he's sane and guilty,' he was reported as saying. 'Maybe he is a danger to foreign women. He must be in prison.'

As it is he has become a media darling, albeit a sick one. 'The public has made me the godfather of cannibalism and I am happy about that,' he says. 'I will always look at the world through the eyes of a cannibal.'

In 1994 he held a one-man seminar called 'Sagawa's World', in which he talked about his desire to eat human flesh and aired a video titled *The Desire to be Eaten*. He played a cult leader in a TV drama, wrote a newspaper column and penned some seven books, one of which was a 1997 commentary on the fourteen-year-old Japanese serial killer known as 'Youth A'. Ironically he also became a restaurant critic for Japanese magazine *Spa*.

To this day he has never expressed regret or remorse for killing and eating Renée. Perhaps he should have been forced to sit down, face to face with her family. Maybe then he would have recognised how damaging and evil it is to take another person's life. But it is doubtful that even that would have prompted any emotion from him.

As he told one magazine, 'My fantasy of cannibalism is not crazy. Everyone has fantasies. The special thing about me is that I acted upon mine.'

In many ways killing Renée was a route to fame. She was sacrificed to allow him to walk on the world stage. Like any sacrificial victim she was dispensable, a means to an end.

TSUTOMU MIYAZAKI

Sagawa might arguably have got off lightly, but fellow countryman and cannibal Tsutomu Miyazaki was not so lucky.

Born on 21 August 1962 in Tokyo, Miyazaki became a bright student with an IQ of 135. But then his grades dropped dramatically and instead of becoming a teacher as he planned, he became a printer's assistant.

His drop in academic achievement might have been down to complications resulting from being born prematurely. He weighed only 4.8 pounds, and the joints in his hands were fused together, making it impossible for him to bend his wrists upwards.

The deformation haunted him from early on. When he was five years old, a classmate teased him about his 'funny hands'. In family photos after that, Miyazaki never showed his hands, and his eyes were often closed.

His teachers and classmates from elementary school recalled him being a quiet, lonely child who seemed incapable of making friends.

As he grew older, he began to stay up into the night, reading comic books.

Due to their careers, Miyazaki's parents had little time for him, while his two younger sisters found him repulsive. Fortunately, his grandfather seemed to take a genuine interest in the boy.

Miyazaki avoided girls his own age, possibly because he was physically immature. 'His penis is no thicker than a pencil and no longer than a toothpick,' one high school classmate remarked. He might not have been well-endowed, but his sex drive was stronger than average.

At college, he took his still and video cameras to the tennis courts to take shots of the female players' crotches. He soon gravitated to porn magazines, but found them wanting. 'They black out the most important part,' he complained. So in 1984 he turned to child porn, which revealed everything – this was down to a strange quirk in Japanese obscenity laws which only banned the showing of pubic hair, not sex organs.

In May 1988 his grandfather died, which devastated

Miyazaki. His grandfather had been his warmest adult relationship; now he felt utterly alone.

Miyazaki later said that he ate some of his grandfather's cremated bones – a claim that Shunsuke Serizawa, a literary critic and witness for Miyazaki's defence, believed. 'He wanted to reincarnate his grandfather, and believed that this reincarnation would not be complete if any of his grandfather's body remained,' he said.

His grandfather's death made him even more distant from the rest of his family. Once, when his youngest sister yelled at him for peeking at her in the bath, he burst in and smashed her head against the bathtub.

Later, when his mother suggested he spend less time watching videos, Miyazaki exploded with rage and beat her up. Miyazaki's father had given up trying to talk to him ages ago.

Three months after his grandfather died, Miyazaki turned to murder.

Shortly after 3pm on 22 August, four-year-old Mari Konno left her home in Saitama, not far from Tokyo, to play at her friend's house. At 6:23pm, after she failed to return, her father, architect Shigeo Konno, struggling to hold his panic in check, called the police to report his daughter missing. About the same time as Konno's phone call, in a dark forest thirty miles away, Mari was being slowly strangled to death by Miyazaki.

Between 1988 and 1989 Miyazaki went on to kill and mutilate three other girls. All his victims were aged between four and seven.

After murdering each girl he had sex with their corpses, and ate portions of flesh from his third and fourth victims. The so-called 'Little Girl Murders' sent shockwaves through Japan.

Miyazaki was a mild-mannered, quiet and obedient employee. No one would have believed he was the monster killing the little girls, whom he selected at random.

Not satisfied with killing and mutilating the girls, Miyazaki went one stage further by terrorising the families of his victims – sending them letters describing in graphic detail what he had done to their children.

And there was worse...

He let the corpse of his first victim, Mari Konno, decompose in the hills near his home, then chopped off the hands and feet, which he kept in his wardrobe. He burnt the remaining bones in a furnace, ground them to powder, and sent them to her family in a box along with some of her teeth, and photos of her clothes. In an accompanying postcard, he wrote, 'Mari. Cremated. Bones. Investigate. Prove.'

Miyazaki was finally apprehended on 23 July 1989. He was trying to insert a zoom lens into the vagina of a schoolgirl in a park close to her home. Her father came along and attacked Miyazaki. He managed to escape, but came back later to pick up his car. Police were waiting for him and arrested him.

When police searched his two-room bungalow they found a collection of 5,763 videos. These included pornographic movies and the first five *Guinea Pig* extreme horror movies. He apparently used the second movie in the series, *Flower of Flesh and Blood*, as a template for one of his murders.

The police also found pictures of his victims amongst the videos.

Miyazaki was found guilty of killing the four girls and

was sentenced to death in 1997 by the Tokyo District Court. The court ruled that he was guilty and sane enough to be held responsible, though he claimed he committed the crimes 'in a dream from which I never woke up'. For him, it was as though he were in a Japanese Studio Ghibli animation – like Hayao Miyazaki's (no relation) award-winning 2001 movie *Spirited Away*, which takes you on a mesmerising trip into a dreamscape so engrossing you begin to wonder whether you will return to your everyday world when you turn off the DVD.

Following his son's conviction, Miyazaki's father, who had refused to pay for his legal defence, committed suicide.

NICOLAS CLAUX

Another cannibal who descended into a nightmare world of unimaginable horror was Nicolas Claux. Like my cannibal informant Eric Soames he got his human flesh from mortuaries and raided graveyards. But unlike Soames he eventually killed to satisfy his deranged lust.

Claux was born in 1972 in Cameroon, Africa. His father, a French citizen, worked in the international finance section of a French bank – a career that required a good deal of travel. When Claux was five the family moved to London. Two years later they were back in their native Paris.

Claux's parents were not short of money, so he didn't want for anything. But as he said himself, 'They never hugged me or kissed me, they just let me be on my own most of the time'. As a result Claux became withdrawn and introverted. 'Eventually I grew emotionally cold,' he recalled later. 'I had difficulties feeling empathy for other people, just indifference most of the time.'

When he was ten years old he got into a heated argument with his grandfather. During the exchange the old man suffered a stroke and fell down dead. This had a profound effect on Claux and led to him becoming obsessed with death. He devoured everything he could on death and the afterlife. He particularly enjoyed books that featured vampires, werewolves, black magic and the occult.

Curiously he also became fascinated by the demon that Eric Soames believed may have possessed internet cannibal Armin Meiwes.

'A photo of the statue of the Sumerian demon Pazuzu especially fascinated me,' Claux remembered. 'I found it in a book my parents had bought in England. For me, it symbolised something extremely ancient and powerful – something that I respected. A few years later, I saw the same statue used in the movie *The Exorcist*, and my interest in the occult grew stronger.'

Pazuzu is usually depicted with the body of a man, the head of a lion or dog, eagle-like taloned feet, two pairs of wings, a scorpion's tail and a serpentine penis. His right hand typically points upwards and his left hand downwards.

As Claux mentions, Pazuzu appears at the beginning of *The Exorcist*. Father Merrin (Max von Sydow in the movie) is at the site of an archaeological dig in Northern Iraq – which was once home to the cultures of Babylonia, Assyria and Sumer – when he sees the menacing sculpted figure of Pazuzu, whom he had battled in an exorcism several years earlier. When Merrin is later appointed to perform an exorcism on a twelve-year-old girl, Regan, he suspects Pazuzu has possessed her.

• • •

POSSESSION

The movie was based on the 1972 novel *The Exorcist* by American writer William Blatty. Although a work of fiction, the inspiration for the book came from a real-life case of apparent demonic possession. This is worth looking at in some detail as it may throw some light on Claux's subsequent need to eat human flesh. It also shows that Eric Soames' belief in demonic possession should not be too quickly dismissed.

None of this is to say that I personally think demons are real; but I do suspect that the concept of external forces like demons and, indeed, angels – famously outlined in mediaeval grimoires (books of black magic) – may well have been a more profound, if poetic, way of describing and mapping the deeper workings of our psyches than psychology is capable of today. It could be that magicians and occultists like Francis Barrett, whose book *The Magus* (1801) outlined a whole system for evoking spirits, angels and demons, were drawing on ancient knowledge about the human mind that has been all but lost in modern times.

Arguably this knowledge could shed greater light on the reasons why some people become cannibals and have unnatural desires to eat human flesh. Modern psychologists attached to police forces try to explain it; but their theories always seem limp and empty. This could well be because they don't want to appear like they are getting into the territory of cranks. You can't blame them; their livelihoods would be at stake if they came anywhere near to discussing notions of possession.

Yet when you look at the story behind the *Exorcist* movie

and book you can see how apparently normal people can behave in the most outlandish and terrifying ways.

In *William Blatty On The Exorcist: From Novel To Film* (1974), Blatty recalls how in 1949 – as a twenty-year-old student at Georgetown University, Washington DC – he heard about a youth from nearby Mount Rainier, Maryland, who had become the victim of demonic possession, and had been cured by a priest. The story was covered by the *Washington Post*, but details were scant. However, it was later established as fact that a fourteen-year-old boy, referred to as Robbie Mannheim or John Hoffman (his real identity is still protected), had an unusual affliction, which had been exacerbated by the death of his aunt Harriet, a self-professed medium, to whom he was very close.

Robbie, an only child, shared his aunt's passion for spiritualism, learning from her how to contact the dead using a Quija board. Whether this accounted for the difficult-to-explain disturbances – such as untraceable dripping – which occurred in the Mannheim home prior to Harriet's death is hard to say. But one thing is certain: shortly after her death on 26 January 1949, the disturbances increased dramatically. Strange scratching noises started coming from the walls of the Mannheim's house and also from within the boy's mattress. Assuming it was rodents, exterminators were called in, but nothing was found, leaving the Mannheims puzzled.

Things then took a sinister turn. Not only did the noises become more frequent, but during the night Robbie would be woken by the violent shaking of his bed, often to find the furniture rearranged around the room. Fearing their property was haunted, the family fled the house and waited for the activity to subside. It soon became clear that the phenomena were not centred on the house, but on Robbie himself; at school, for example, his desk, reportedly, moved around the classroom as if it were on wheels.

Robbie's health also appeared to deteriorate. He began to complain of internal pains and would lapse into blackouts. During the blackouts, the psychokinetic phenomena became particularly intense; amongst other things, fruit and ornaments would fly around the house. Later, Robbie started to babble incoherently while he was unconscious; he also became violent and eventually had to be put under restraint. Doctors could not offer a diagnosis. A physics professor, having witnessed Robbie's bedside table levitate, could only say, 'There is much we have yet to discover concerning the nature of electromagnetism.'

Concluding that Robbie was possessed, in all probability by Aunt Harriet, the family tried ordering the entity to leave. It didn't. What's more, it soon began to look as if several personalities were now lurking within Robbie's troubled psyche. In desperation, the family contacted their Lutheran minister, the Reverend Schulze. He didn't believe in demonic possession. But when Robbie stayed overnight at his house and he witnessed Robbie's bed shaking and a heavy armchair moving of its own volition, Shulze told the Mannheims, 'You have to see a Catholic priest. The Catholics know about things like this.'

The Mannheims followed this advice and soon after were visited by Father E. Albert Hughes. On seeing the priest, Robbie immediately became vicious and obscene. Interestingly, when Hughes heard Robbie's 'incoherent babble', he recognised it as Latin, a language the boy had never studied. At one point, Robbie stated in Latin: 'O Sacerdos Christi, tu scis me esse diabolim' (Oh Priest of Christ, you know that I am the Devil).

By 27 February, Robbie had been admitted to the Jesuit-run Georgetown University Hospital and the twenty-nine-year-old Hughes, having obtained official sanction from the Catholic Church, set about exorcising the boy.

He failed. On 4 March, after five nights, the exorcism – performed according to the dictates of the Rituale Romanum liturgy of 1614 – came to an abrupt end when Robbie worked a bedspring free and sliced Hughes down the length of his arm. The wound, requiring 100 stitches, permanently disabled the priest, leaving him unable to perform Mass unaided again.

Perhaps because the exorcism was a failure, Hughes' involvement with the case was not revealed publicly and the Catholic Church decreed that all records concerning the exorcism be sealed. Hughes himself refused for years to talk about the exorcism, even to colleagues.

Towards the end of his life, however, he talked through the events with his curate, Father Frank Bober. 'Speaking in tongues, levitation, puking, he said all that was valid,' recalls Bober. 'There are some things that you just can't explain medically, because the boy supposedly not only spoke Latin but ancient Aramaic and ancient Hebrew – I mean, languages you don't just pick up.'

After the failure of Hughes's exorcism, the Mannheim family went to stay with relatives in St Louis, where another priest was consulted – the fifty-two-year-old, and more worldly, William Bowdern. He had Robbie placed in a secure ward at the Alexian Brothers Hospital and

Left: Albert Fish, also known as the Werewolf of Wysteria, who confessed to eating one of his victims, Billy Gaffney, in the following way: 'I made a stew out of his ears, nose, pieces of his face and belly. I put onions, carrots, turnips, celery, salt and pepper [sic]. It was good.'

Right: A late-starter in cannibal terms, Andrei Chikatilo was in his forties when he committed his first murder. He made up for lost time, however, by going on to murder at least 52 women and children.

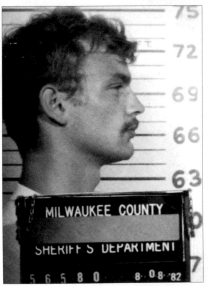

Top: Armin Meiwes (*left*), who famously exploited the world wide web to advertise his interest in eating human flesh, finding a willing victim in the form of Bernd Brandes (*right*).

Below: Necrophiliac cannibal Jeffrey Dahmer, one of the most notorious serial killers of modern times.

Left: Ed Gein. Although not as prolific as others of his ilk, his use of the skins of his victims to create an array of macabre household decorations ensured his infamous place in history.

Right: Gary Heidnik, whose depraved imprisonment and torture of six women in 1986-7 involved feeding the remains of one of his victims to the others. He was, however, to keep the ribcage and head for himself...

J. Nicholls delin. J. Bavire sculp.

SAWNEY BEANE at the Entrance of his Cave

The most prolific cannibal ever? Or no more than a mere myth? Whichever, Sawney Bean and his ghastly cave of horrors (where his victims would provide a communal supper for his family) continue to live on in the public imagination.

assisted by fellow priests Raymond Bishop and Walter Halloran, Bowdern set about exorcising the boy. Despite their best efforts, Robbie's condition became even more inexplicable, with blotched 'writing' manifesting on his skin, starting with the word "Hell" and going on to more complex messages.

After gaining permission from his archbishop, Bowdern began a further exorcism and was subjected to a barrage of projectile vomiting, flung excreta, and obscene taunting. Even worse, the young Father Halloran, an athlete, suffered a broken nose while trying to hold Robbie down. The ritual continued for four weeks. Then finally, on the night of 18 April, Saint Michael apparently entered into Robbie. 'Satan! I am Saint Michael,' announced Robbie/Saint Michael. 'And I command you, Satan, and the other evil spirits, to leave this body in the name of Dominus. Immediately! Now! Now! Now!'

At this, Robbie's symptoms abruptly vanished. To be certain this was not more devilish trickery, Bowdern asked for a sign to confirm the success of the exorcism and a sound like a gunshot echoed through the corridors of the hospital. Robbie was duly dispatched home.

The story did not end there. In 1978, when a wing of the Alexian Brothers Hospital was to be demolished, workmen prized open the door to a fifth-floor room in the wing for the seriously disturbed. It had not been occupied in the twenty-nine years since the exorcism, having induced spasms of fear in several people. In the drawer of the bedside table, a faded diary was found, containing a record of what happened in 1949. This was given to Father Halloran, by then the only surviving priest from the exorcism conducted there. In 1988, he gave an interview to the *Lincoln Star*, Nebraska, finally revealing all.

Washington-based author, Thomas B. Allen, saw the story and decided to follow up the case. After locating Halloran (by then ailing in a retirement home), he pieced together his book, *Possessed: The True Story of an Exorcism*, the definitive study of the case. 'He (Halloran) felt that he had actually fought with the Devil,' says Allen, 'and he wanted subsequent exorcists to have something to go on.'

What are we to make of that? Although it is a highly compelling story, none of it should be taken as proof that the Devil or other dark entities exist in the sense that, say, a horse or a cow does. But it could lead us to suspect that the human mind is far vaster than modern psychology would have us believe. And that, given the right circumstances, certain aspects of our deeper minds, which ideally should stay hidden, can spring to the surface and lead some people to do terrifying, almost inhuman things – as though they are possessed.

All the cannibals we've seen so far have become almost inhuman in their attitudes and demeanour. Armin Meiwes kept some of his humanity in that he only wanted willing victims to kill and eat, but he still prowled the internet looking to satisfy his savage lusts. Peter Bryan simply became a beast that saw humans as nothing more than meat. Issei Sagawa had no hesitation in gunning down Renée Hartevelt, eating parts of her flesh and having sex with her corpse. It is as if he became a grotesque demon feeding on the flesh of his own kind, expressing a dark sexuality that would drive most of us insane if forced to watch such a spectacle.

But Robbie Mannheim – who admittedly wasn't a cannibal but did behave in a terrifying manner – seemed like an ordinary boy until his aunt died. It could be that his dabbling with the Ouija board, combined with the death of his aunt, to whom he was close, opened the gates for malefic forces to enter. Soames, of course, would say that these forces were real demonic entities. But the gates that opened could just as easily have been purely in his mind. Opening these gates could have had the same effect as dropping a tab of LSD would have done. But instead of opening the 'doors of perception', the gates of hell itself swung open...

The same kind of thing could be happening in cases of cannibals who kill.

In the case of Nicolas Claux, the death of his grandfather and his obsession with the Babylonian demon Pazuzu could have been the catalysts that opened parts of his psyche that should remain sealed. They allowed the evil genie to leap out and take Claux on a chilling odyssey of flesh eating.

INTO THE CRYPT

At the age of twelve, Claux and his parents moved to Lisbon, Portugal, where they stayed for four years. The setting had changed but his obsession with death and the occult simply got stronger. None of his classmates shared his interests, so once again he was without friends. As his loneliness grew he began to hate everyone around him.

On moving back to Paris at sixteen, Claux took to wandering through the elaborate graves and crypts of Parisian cemeteries. Between 1990 and 1993 he came to know these places of the dead like the back of his hand. 'As a botanist studies plants and flowers, I would examine rusty locks and evaluate the weight of cement lids,' he said. 'My favourite things were mausoleums. The most impressive ones can be found at Pere-Lachaise, Montmartre or Passy cemeteries. I would peek through their windows to see the inside. Some were decorated with furniture, paintings, or statues. It was not long before I began working on a plan to get a much closer view.'

He needed to get inside and get closer to the dead.

Using lock-picks and crowbars – or breaking in through windows if need be – Claux began to explore the mausoleums that fascinated him most. Once inside, he said he 'felt like an emperor reigning in Hell'. At last he had found a place where he belonged – a kingdom of the damned. Often he would break into a tomb during the day, then resurface at night when the gates were closed. That way he could continue his activities without fear of being discovered.

In the end, just sitting staring at coffins wasn't enough. He needed to take his obsession further.

I woke up one day feeling this sinister urge to dig up a corpse and mutilate it. I gathered a small crowbar, a pair of pliers, a screwdriver, black candles and a pair of surgical gloves in a backpack. Then I took the metro [to] the Trocadero station. It was nearly noon. The gates of the Passy Cemetery were wide open, but nobody was inside. The undertakers were out for lunch.

Built during the nineteenth century, Passy is a small gothic graveyard, with lots of large mausoleums. The composer Claude Debussy (1862–1918) is buried there, as is impressionist painter Édouard Manet (1832–1883). It is located between two large avenues, which would have made it difficult for Claux to climb in at night. But he concluded that nobody was likely to suspect anyone of grave robbing at noon.

I had this special grave in mind. It was a small mausoleum, the burial site of a family or Russian immigrants from the 1917 revolution. I had already prised open the iron door a few days before, and I had closed it afterwards so it would seem that nobody had ever touched it. All I had to do was kick it open..., At this point, my mind was in total chaos. I had flashes of death in my head. I took a deep breath, and I climbed down the steps leading to the crypt.

The crypt was dank and dark. But he'd brought candles along to illuminate the scene. He carefully removed one of the heavy coffins from its stone casing. Then he unscrewed the lid and removed it using a crowbar.

Once opened, a horrible stench of putrefaction came out of the box... Then I saw the body inside. It was a half-rotten old woman, shrouded in a white sheet, covered with brown stains. Her face seemed to be smeared with oil, but it was simply the death fluids oozing from her skin. The stench was so intense that I nearly fainted. The teeth were protruding from the mouth, but her eyes were gone. I stared into the empty eye sockets, and all of a sudden something broke into my mind.

That's when he picked up a screwdriver, and...

...the corpse inside the coffin started to move slightly, like it had guessed what would happen next. So I began to stab the belly, the rib area and the shoulders. I stabbed her at least fifty times. I really can't remember. All I can remember is that when I woke up my forearms covered with corpse slime. I tried to sever her head, but I did not have the right tools. I took Polaroid snapshots [of the corpse].

After violating his first grave, Nicolas spent much of his free time searching the cemetery for new graves to desecrate. He also took to collecting souvenirs from the tombs he raided, which he took back to his apartment. 'Throughout my apartment, bone fragments and human teeth were scattered about like loose change; vertebrae and leg bones hung from the ceiling like morbid mobiles,' he said.

In 1992, at twenty, Claux joined the army, where he trained as a gunsmith, cleaning and repairing weapons. But he found it unfulfilling. He needed a job that would bring him into direct contact with death. So he took the logical step and applied to train as a mortician. After being turned down he got a job as a morgue attendant at St Vincent-de-Paul's children's hospital in Paris.

I found that it was the best way to be in contact with corpses. My first contact with a corpse there was when I assisted the autopsy of a ten-year-old girl. The other attendant showed me how to stitch up her belly, and that was the first time I ever got to touch a fresh corpse. I was amazed by how red and clean her organs were.

CANNIBALS

He didn't stay at St Vincent-de-Paul's for long. In December 1993 he took a similar position as a morgue attendant and stretcher-bearer at Saint Joseph's Hospital, in Paris. His duties involved helping with autopsies, cleaning up the morgue slabs, and preparing the bodies for wakes.

Most of the autopsies were done by us, the morgue attendants. We would do the Y-shaped incision, cut the ribs at the joints, and open the skull with an electric saw. The pathologist only dissected the organs and put them in a box.

I would be left alone with the body after the autopsy to do the stitches, which were my specialty. This is when I began eating strips of muscles from the bodies. I always checked out their medical files first. I talked with a butcher once who told me that meat is better three or four days after death. This was something I had always dreamed of doing, and it was the opportunity to do it on a regular basis.

Sometimes I brought select meats home with me to be cooked, but my preference was to eat them raw. It tasted like tartar steak, or carpaccio. The big muscles of the thighs and back were good, but there was no good meat in the breasts, only fats. People often ask me what went through my mind the first time I indulged my cannibalistic fantasy. Well, to be honest, I said to myself: 'Wow! Now I'm a cannibal. Cool!'

Besides working in the morgue, his job included delivering blood from the hospital blood bank to the operating theatres. It didn't take him long to notice that blood bags were often left unused. Eventually he came up with a scheme for pilfering them. He would take the sticker off the unused bag, making it look like it had been opened. When no one was looking he would stash it in his locker. At the end of his shift he simply slipped it in his backpack, took it home, and put it in his fridge to cool. He then added protein powders or human ashes to the blood and drank it. Because there was no plasma in the bags, the blood was very thin, which was why he thickened it.

Yet again Claux became dissatisfied. Eating human flesh and drinking blood wasn't enough for him. He'd even got a girlfriend who liked being beaten, but the edge had gone from that too. He needed to take his obsession to its ultimate conclusion and kill someone.

Claux chose 4 October 1994 to turn his fantasies into reality. He spent the morning searching for a victim, any victim. He really didn't care. He wasn't bothered about their age, race or sex. All he wanted to do was kill someone. Had you been walking around Paris that day, you might well have become Claux's victim. It was random. There was a killer on the loose, but no one knew.

As it was – out of a city teeming with people – he couldn't find anyone who took his fancy. So by early afternoon he gave up.

Then an idea occurred to him. Why not try his luck on Minitel? It was an early version of the Internet, much used by gays and people into S&M to arrange meetings. What's more, that summer and autumn there had been a series of murders of gay men, which had left the police baffled. One more murder, Claux reasoned, wouldn't make a lot of difference and the blame would likely be put on whoever the killer was. He stood to be able to fulfil his fantasy and get off scot free.

But there was a downside. 'Queers were an easy prey,' said Claux, 'but the bad side was that I couldn't mutilate them and eat some of their meat, because I don't like to touch men, and they have diseases.'

Nevertheless he logged on to Minitel and soon began chatting with Thierry Bissonnier, a thirty-year-old restaurateur and classical musician, about bondage and S&M. He was involved with an older man, but presumably enjoyed the odd session of anonymous sex. After exchanging a few emails the two decided it would be good to get together and Bissonnier gave Claux his address. This is how Claux later described the meeting to police:

So I agreed on meeting Thierry around noon. With me I carried a single shot .22 calibre handgun, which I hid under my jacket. When I arrived at his place, a one-room apartment under the roof of an old building, I knocked on the door and gave him the fake first name that I had given him on Minitel. He opened the door, I stepped inside, quickly turned around while he was closing the door and pulled out the gun.

I looked at his face just as he turned his head towards me and saw the gun pointed at his eye. After a few awkward moments passed, I pulled the trigger. He instantly fell face down without a word. It was really eerie. It all happened like in slow motion. Then I watched him bleed on the carpet. Soon I decided to see what the apartment was like and wandered around a bit.

When I returned to where he was lying I observed that he was still moving and making horrible breathing noises on the floor, like if he was breathing through a straw. I reloaded the gun and shot again, this time striking him in the back of the head. I reloaded and fired a few more times, but he was still alive and making noise. I was surprised that he was still holding on, I had expected the first shot to kill him.

After a few minutes, I went into his kitchen and found some cookies to eat and then sat in a corner of the room and watched him as I ate. When I was finished, I decided to get out of there quickly, so I shot him one last time in the back. I also lifted a huge plant container and smashed it on his head, crushing it some. I then wiped down my fingerprints; picked up his chequebook; a credit card and a wallet (with ID papers); his driving licence; an alarm clock, and an answering machine, and finally left the scene.

Bissonnier's body wasn't discovered for three days. His parents, worried when he didn't return their calls, went to his apartment and found the grisly remains of their son's body decomposing on the floor. One of the first investigators on the scene was Chief Inspector Gilbert Thiel. It looked like yet another gay murder. That month alone there had been seven others in almost identical circumstances.

In Paris at the time homosexual murders represented around a third of all murders in the city. They were easy prey because they indulged in risky behaviour, such as meeting people they hardly knew for sex, often without telling anyone where they were going. During the early 1990s, the majority of gay sex encounters began with messages on Minitel.

The autopsy report on Bissonnier showed that the first bullet entered his eyeball, stopping just short of the brain. The next few rounds were stopped by his skull, except one which slightly penetrated his brain. The final shot entered through his back and pierced his heart, killing him almost instantly.

Now the police had to work out who murdered him – and why. At first they thought Bissonnier had been killed by whomever was behind the other gay murders in the city – as Claux had hoped. But then they realised there were subtle differences between the other gay murders and the Bissonnier killing. There was no sexual mutilation and the body hadn't been violated like in most of the other cases. And the robbery seemed a bit half-hearted; easily saleable items had been left in the apartment.

It seemed that neither hate-crime nor robbery were the motive. So what was? Why had Thierry Bissonnier been shot down in cold blood?

The answer might never have been known if Claux hadn't made a fatal mistake. If it hadn't been for this he probably would have got away with the random killing, which was essentially done for kicks like the extreme violence committed by Alex and his gang of 'droogs' in the Anthony Burgess novel, *Clockwork Orange* (1962), later made into a movie by Stanley Kubrick.

Claux's error was to try to forge one of Bissonnier's cheques to buy a new video recorder. He needed to give the shop assistant some form of ID. So he handed over

Bissonnier's driving licence, ineptly doctored with his own photograph. The attempted scam was soon foiled when Claux made a botched job of forging Bissonnier's signature. The cops were called. Claux panicked and ran off, leaving the driving licence with his picture on it.

Investigators now had something to go on. They were looking for a young guy with long, black hair and a small beard in connection with the murder of Bissonnier.

But they didn't know who he was. A stroke of luck, however, delivered Claux straight into the hands of police. On 15 November 1994, six weeks after the killing, he got into a heated row with a woman outside the famous Moulin Rouge nightclub. A passing cop intervened to break up the argument, which had got out of hand. He took one look at Claux and immediately recognised his face. He was the guy in the forged driving licence photo that had been circulated around Paris Metropolitan Police department.

Claux was arrested and taken to the police station. Detectives wasted no time in heading over to his apartment and conducting a thorough search of its macabre contents. They sifted through his collection of human bones, teeth, graveyard dirt and slasher videos. Under his bed they found a .22 calibre pistol.

Meanwhile, back at the station, Claux was denying all knowledge of Bissonnier's death. But when ballistic tests on the gun brought a match with the bullets found in Bissonnier, Claux had no option but to confess.

Further investigation revealed he had been robbing graves in several Parisian gothic graveyards, stealing the bones and mutilating the mummified remains. Police then asked Claux why he was storing blood bags in his fridge. 'I simply answered that I drank it on a regular basis,' he recalled later. 'I also confessed to being on a very special diet and went on to describe my mortuary job and the cannibalism.'

Detectives were keen to discover his motive for the killing. At first Claux claimed it was a simple robbery that had gone badly wrong. They didn't buy it. The way they saw it there had been too much overkill; Claux had pumped Bissonnier full of bullets. Yet the first shot would have been enough for Claux to make his escape if Bissonnier had simply caught him in the act of robbing his apartment. Then there was the meticulous way Claux had removed his fingerprints...

Everything pointed to a more sinister motive. Then Claux revised his position, saying the murder had been an act of revenge taken out on a random homosexual after an argument with another gay man.

Unconvinced, police asked him if his motive had been sexual, what with the victim being homosexual? Claux insisted it wasn't. It then struck him that coming clean about his motives might work in his favour. He might get a lesser sentence on the grounds of diminished responsibility. Considering his background, claiming temporary insanity was not exactly going to be hard for the legal system to swallow.

So he told police, 'I was just looking for death,' and explained that he drank blood because he believed he was a vampire.

For two years after his arrest Claux was kept in the Fleury-Merogis jail. While the police were busy constructing a watertight case against him, Claux was put through extensive psychological tests. It was concluded that he was psychotic with a bent for necrophilia (he apparently had sex with some of the corpses in the morgue where he worked) and sadism. Further testing revealed he had the typical symptoms of a schizophrenic personality.

By December 1996 the police decided they had enough evidence to bring Claux to book for premeditated murder, and handed the case over to the Office of Prosecution.

Claux's trial began on 9 May 1997. The presiding judge imposed a news blackout on the case so exact details of the proceedings aren't known. But Claux's defence counsel entered a plea of not guilty on his behalf. The prosecution countered by displaying photos of the crime scene, Bissonnier's body and of Claux's macabre apartment, saying that his lifestyle revealed a highly morbid and violent personality. They then described him as a 'death addict' and 'real-life vampire'.

The prosecution also tried to link Claux to the other gay murders that had gone on in the city before his arrest, despite the fact that there was no physical evidence connecting him to them. All they'd got was a number of witnesses who claimed they'd seen Claux in gay bars that had been frequented by some of the victims – and the fact that Claux's psychological profile matched that of a serial killer.

The nine-strong jury deliberated for three hours. Then found Claux guilty of premeditated murder, armed robbery, fraudulent use of a cheque, falsification of a driving licence and of fraudulently attempting to buy a video recorder. He was sentenced to twelve years in prison.

Two years went by and he was sent to Maison Centrale Poissy maximum security prison where he used his time productively, studying computer programming and taking up painting, which it turned out he had a natural talent for.

He was released on 12 March 2002, having served only seven years and four months of his sentence. Making the most of his freedom he travelled in Sweden and England before settling down again in Paris. Once he'd found his feet it was time to think about making a living. Clearly he could have gone down the road of low-paid menial jobs, like most ex-cons end up doing. But the obvious thing to do was capitalise on what he'd done; after all, his crimes had enormous publicity value.

Claux reasoned that in our celebrity-dominated world even murderers and serial killers can become famous (or rather notorious, but it amounts to the same thing). The fact that you've murdered someone seemed to be of no consequence, except of course to the victims and their families.

So Claux immediately got down to publicising himself. He dubbed himself the 'Vampire of Paris' and advertised his morbid and murderous past life on the internet. He also set up a website at http://nicoclaux.free.fr to sell his paintings which include scenes of autopsies and portraits of notorious serial killers and cannibals. Eventually he became a regular guest on TV and radio chat shows relating tales about his dark past as a killer and grave robber.

His big coup, revenue-wise, came in 2006 when a US company began marketing a 2007 calendar showcasing his paintings. Demand was such that a 2008 edition went in to production, along with a line of posters (see www.serialkillercalendar.com).

It might be sick. But at least Claux isn't living off the state and claiming benefits like so many ex-cons tend to do.

He also regularly attends goth and vampire conventions, giving talks on his former life and selling his paintings to the appreciative crowds. He might have been a lonely and friendless child, but now he's got a hectic social life and a steady girlfriend. Claux says he spends his time 'painting, watching horror flicks, working out and writing to other killers, plus watching documentaries on freaks or amputees'.

He claims to worship the Devil. But that can hardly be held against him, especially when you consider the horrendous atrocities committed in the name of Christianity over the years. And besides, the majority of Satanists are upstanding citizens. So there's no reason Claux shouldn't be too, so long as he's put his past behind him as he claims to have done.

Of course, his victim's friends and family would not agree. But maybe Bissonnier was in some way destined to be a sacrificial lamb. Maybe all murder victims are. Maybe the killers are equally destined to wield the 'sacrificial knife'. And maybe there is nothing we can do about it...

FIVE:
FULL MOON FEVER

MOON-STRUCK

According to legend, full moon is the time when werewolves come out. They howl at the silvery orb as it rises in the night sky, then seek out a victim whom they tear to pieces with their razor sharp fangs. Most people would dismiss this as an old wives' tale. But there is a lot of truth in old legends, especially if you look for the metaphorical meaning behind werewolves and other mythical creatures.

Full moon is a very powerful time. If you look up at it and quiet your thoughts for a moment you'll sense that the atmosphere is somehow different to how it has been during the rest of the month. You might even feel that strange forces could be abroad.

Magicians and witches have long followed the phases of the moon. They recognise that the waxing moon is a good time to perform spells for gain and attraction; while the waning moon is good for workings of lessening and banishing. But they also know that certain invisible forces come to the fore at full moon, and also during the dark of the moon.

Scientists, of course, tell us that the moon affects the tides and, to an extent, animals. But they usually draw the line at it affecting human behaviour to any extent.

Yet police in Toledo, Ohio, claim that crime rises by five per cent during nights with a full moon. Police in Kentucky have also laid the blame on the full moon for temporary rises in crime. In Britain, a survey conducted by an insurance group in 2003 found that car accidents rise by up to 50 per cent during full moons compared to the time of the new moon. In the Midlands there was a 13 per cent rise in all types of accident, ranging from multi-vehicle pile-ups to single car collisions and reversing into lamp posts.

In June 2007 senior police officers in Brighton announced that they were planning to deploy more officers over the summer to counter trouble they believe is linked to the lunar cycle. They said the peak of the lunar cycle – full moon – seems to attract violent yobs. Metaphorically speaking they turn into werewolves.

'I compared a graph of full moons and a graph of last year's violent crimes and there is a trend,' said Inspector Andy Parr, who oversees the policing of Brighton's pubs and clubs. 'People tend to be more aggressive generally.'

Research published in early 2007 by Michael Zimecki of the Polish Academy of Sciences claimed to have found a link between lunar cycles and criminality. Other studies dismiss the idea.

But as another spokesperson for the Brighton police said, 'We're not saying this is scientific. It's an old wives' tale, but perhaps there's something in it? Is it a coincidence or is there something more to it?'

ALBERT FISH

There was a full moon on the ill-fated night of 3 June 1928 when a kindly-looking middle-aged man called Albert Fish went to visit the Budds at their home in New York for dinner. Whether it had any specific effect on the troubled psyche of Fish is open to debate. But he was certainly out hunting for prey – human prey. He might not have looked like a werewolf, but he certainly behaved like one – and was even once dubbed the 'Werewolf of Wisteria'.

He'd first visited the Budds on 28 May. They lived in the deprived Chelsea district of Manhattan. A few days previously the Budd's son Edward was looking for work and had placed a classified advert in the Sunday edition of the New York World newspaper. It read: 'Young man, 18, wishes position in country. Edward Budd, 406 West 15th Street.' His father, Albert, was finding it hard to support his wife and four children on his wage as a porter for the Equitable Life Assurance Society. So Edward was looking to do his bit to help out.

Fish, then fifty-eight, saw the ad and went round to visit the Budds on the pretext of hiring Edward. He introduced himself as Frank Howard, a farmer from Farmingdale, Long Island. He told Edward he was willing to pay him fifteen dollars a week if he was prepared to work hard. The family were delighted at the offer. The mild-mannered man said he would return a week later for a firm decision.

He failed to keep the appointment, but sent a telegram apologising for having been unavoidably delayed. As it was, he arrived the next day, Sunday 3 June. He was bearing gifts this time too. He handed Albert's wife, Delia, a pot of soft cheese and a box of strawberries, explaining they were produce from his farm. He was smartly dressed and flashed a wallet stuffed with money – a rarity in the poverty-stricken late twenties in New York.

He seemed more than above board.

Fish had dinner with the family, then gave the older children money to go to the movies. His initial interest had been Edward Budd, but he turned out to be a big strapping young man – not exactly easy to overpower. A change of plan was in order and he turned his attention to the Budd's ten-year-old daughter Grace.

He said he was about to go to a birthday party at the house of his married sister at 137th Street off Columbus Avenue, matter-of-factly suggesting that Grace might like to come along.

The parents gave their permission. Albert said that she didn't see too many 'good times' and that this was a good opportunity.

In her white communion dress, Grace trustingly took Fish's hand and was led away, never to be seen alive again.

After Grace failed to return home, the Budds called the police. A few quick checks showed that the address Fish gave for his sister's house didn't exist; Columbus Avenue only went as far as 109th Street. Further enquiries brought the chilling news that there was no 'Frank Howard' who owned a farm in Long Island. Nor was there any clue as to who he really was. Fish had been cunning; he'd taken back the telegram he sent to the Budd family.

Detective Will King of the Missing Persons Bureau was determined to find Grace. After mounting a huge search of records he found out that the telegram had been sent from the East Harlem branch of Western Union. But this wasn't a lot of use. To have made any headway the police would have had to have searched every house and apartment in East Harlem. It was a big area; they simply didn't have the resources to do it.

King's next move was to track down where the pot of soft cheese had been purchased. Every store in Harlem was visited and eliminated before he found the street trader who had sold it. He was able to give an accurate description of Fish, but this didn't bring police any closer to being able to apprehend him.

There was a good deal of newspaper and radio coverage about the abducted child. This brought lots of crank calls, but no real clues. As the months went by the search proved hopeless and the police were forced to turn their attention to the other crimes that were going on in the city. Detective King, however, refused to give up hope and remained determined to find Grace or her killer (he didn't expect to find her alive).

Seven years later, in November 1934, Fish sent a letter to Delia Budd, which proved his undoing. Thankfully Mrs Budd was illiterate and couldn't read the shockingly sadistic nature of the contents, which could have come straight out of the pages of a Marquis de Sade story. Instead her son Edward, now twenty-five, read it. This is what Fish wrote, complete with misspellings and poor grammar:

My Dear Mrs. Budd.
In 1894 a friend of mine shipped as a deck hand on the

Steamer Tacoma, Capt. John Davis. They sailed from San Francisco for Hong Kong, China. On arriving there he and two others went ashore and got drunk. When they returned the boat was gone.

At that time there was famine in China. Meat of any kind was from $1–3 per pound. So great was the suffering among the very poor that all children under 12 were sold for food in order to keep others from starving. A boy or girl under 14 was not safe in the street. You could go in any shop and ask for steak – chops – or stew meat.

Part of the naked body of a boy or girl would be brought out and just what you wanted cut from it. A boy or girl's behind which is the sweetest part of the body and sold as veal cutlet brought the highest price.

John stayed there so long he acquired a taste for human flesh. On his return to N.Y. he stole two boys, one seven and one eleven. Took them to his home stripped them naked tied them in a closet. Then burned everything they had on. Several times every day and night he spanked them – tortured them – to make their meat good and tender.

First he killed the eleven year old boy, because he had the fattest ass and of course the most meat on it. Every part of his body was cooked and eaten except the head – bones and guts. He was roasted in the oven (all of his ass), boiled, broiled, fried and stewed. The little boy was next, went the same way. At that time, I was living at 409 E 100 St. near – right side. He told me so often how good human flesh was I made up my mind to taste it.

CANNIBALS

On Sunday June the 3, 1928 I called on you at 406 W 15 St. Brought you pot cheese – strawberries. We had lunch. Grace sat in my lap and kissed me. I made up my mind to eat her. On the pretence of taking her to a party. You said yes she could go. I took her to an empty house in Westchester I had already picked out.

When we got there, I told her to remain outside. She picked wildflowers. I went upstairs and stripped all my clothes off. I knew if I did not I would get her blood on them. When all was ready I went to the window and called her. Then I hid in a closet until she was in the room. When she saw me all naked she began to cry and tried to run down the stairs. I grabbed her and she said she would tell her mamma.

First I stripped her naked. How she did kick – bite and scratch. I choked her to death, then cut her in small pieces so I could take my meat to my rooms. Cook and eat it. How sweet and tender her little ass was roasted in the oven. It took me 9 days to eat her entire body. I did not fuck her though I could of had I wished. She died a virgin.

When Edward finished reading he ran straight to the police – in a fury. Detective Will King was still on the case. His dedication to tracking down Grace's killer was such that he had declined to retire two years earlier.

Now, after all these years, he'd got a second clue. The first had been the telegram form signed 'Howard'. The handwriting matched the letter. It was the same man.

King also noticed that the envelope was imprinted with the letters NYPCBA inside a hexagonal shield. This turned out to be the logo of the New York Private Chauffeurs

Benevolent Association. The police checked through the Association's membership cards to try and find a match with the handwriting on the letter. None of the over four hundred samples matched.

King then assembled the employees and asked if any of them had taken the Association's stationery for personal use?

A janitor at the Association, Lee Siscoski, admitted he had, saying he'd left some sheets of stationery in a room he used to rent at 200 West 52nd Street. When King described 'Howard' to the landlady of the boarding house, she nodded in recognition, 'Yes, that sounds like the man in number seven, Albert Fish.'

Fish's signature on the register matched the handwriting of the man who had written both the telegram and the letter. It looked like they'd got their man. The only problem was he'd moved on. But the landlady said he would be back at some point to collect the monthly cheque sent to him by one of his sons.

Ever determined to bring the killer to book, King rented a room in the boarding house and sat down to wait...

Three weeks later Fish arrived. When King confronted him, Fish lunged at him with a cut-throat razor, slashing maniacally at him. King moved quickly out of reach, then grabbed Fish's arm and smashed it against the wall to disarm him. He then cuffed him and led him to the station.

After his initial attack Fish was no trouble and fully co-operated with police.

He confessed to Grace's murder and described it in detail.

He told police how, shortly before visiting the Budd's for dinner, he had gone to a pawnbrokers in Manhattan and bought a meat cleaver, saw and butcher's knife. He wrapped them in a brown paper parcel which he left at a newsagents, saying he would pick it up later. On his return he had Grace by his side. He picked up the parcel and the two of them took the train to Greenburgh in Westchester County. 'We'll soon be there,' he told the smiling Grace who thought she was going to a birthday party at his sister's house.

After getting off the train they walked to a broken-down house called 'Wisteria Cottage', which backed on to some woods. Fish suggested Grace go and pick some flowers while he looked to see where his sister was.

Once inside Fish went upstairs and laid out his butchering tools, which he later described as his 'implements of Hell'. He then stripped off all his clothes and called Grace inside. When she saw him naked she screamed, 'I'll tell Mama!' The fevered Fish leapt on the terrified child, strangling her as she struggled desperately to escape his clutches. Finally she was dead.

Then, in a frenzy of excitement, he hacked her small body to pieces. After putting her head in an outside toilet he got dressed and wrapped up a few of Grace's body parts in a cloth to take home with him.

Once back, he cooked them up with vegetables in a stew. For nine days he made return visits to Wisteria Cottage and returned with more body parts to eat.

As he ate them – and even when he imagined eating them – he would get sexually excited, taking his erect penis in hand to masturbate himself to orgasm.

When he was done, he threw the little that remained of Grace's body over a wall at the back of the cottage.

When asked by a dumbfounded policeman why he had done it, Fish said, 'It occurred to me.'

• • •

Fish's confession didn't end with Grace. He went on to tell police about four hundred other child murders he had committed between 1910 and 1934. A lot of what Fish told police proved to be grossly exaggerated or plain lies. But he had committed a string of child murders in various states, and had a criminal record stretching back to 1903, when he served sixteen months in Sing Sing prison on a grand larceny charge.

What came as a shock to police was he had also been arrested six times since the disappearance of Grace on charges ranging from petty theft to sending obscene letters through the post. They'd had Grace's killer in their hands, but didn't know it.

Fish did have a difficult childhood, which could explain his subsequent actions. But it should always be borne in mind that children in war-torn countries in the developing world arguably have much more difficult childhoods than Fish did, yet we don't see hundreds of thousands of cannibalistic serial killers coming out of places like Africa, Afghanistan and Iraq.

Albert Fish was born on 10 May 1870 in Washington, DC. He was originally named 'Hamilton' Fish, but he later changed it to Albert after other kids kept calling him by the nickname 'Ham and Eggs'.

His father Randall (1795–1875) was forty-three years older than his mother and had been a riverboat captain, but by the time his son was born he was a fertiliser manufacturer. Fish had three older siblings – Walter, Annie and Edwin.

It was a respectable enough family, but there was a streak of mental illness running through it – two relatives died in institutions and one suffered from religious mania.

Fish's father died in 1875, and young Albert's mother

was eventually forced to place him in an orphanage due to lack of money. He was regularly beaten and whipped there, but soon discovered he enjoyed physical pain to the point that he would get an erection, which the other boys teased him about.

By 1879 his mother had got a government job and was in a position to look after him again. But the damage seemed to have been done. Referring to his experiences in the orphanage Fish later said, '... it ruined my mind'.

In 1882, at the age of twelve, Fish began a gay relationship with a telegraph boy, who also introduced him to the delights of drinking urine and coprophagia (eating faeces). At this time Fish spent much of his weekends visiting public baths where he would watch boys undress.

In 1890 he went to live in New York, where he said he became a male prostitute. He also claimed he raped young boys, a crime he kept up even after he got married in 1898 to a girl of nineteen (Fish was twenty-eight). The marriage brought six children – Albert, Anna, Gertrude, Eugene, John and Henry – and Fish worked as a painter and decorator to support the family.

Fish apparently never harmed any of his children. At Fish's later trial for murder his daughter Gertrude, by then in her thirties, recalled how he always said Grace before every meal, read the Bible and attended church regularly. As far as she could remember, Fish had never struck any of the children.

But they were aware of his weird behaviour. He would regularly climb to the top of a hill near their home in Westchester County, New York, strip naked and howl at the moon, screaming, 'I am Christ! I am Christ!' Even then he was obsessed with flesh eating. He collected newspaper articles on cannibalism, which he kept with him until they turned yellow in his pockets; he also served up raw meat to his children on nights when the moon was full.

Other odd behaviour included burning himself with pokers, inserting needles into his groin and whipping himself with a nail-studded paddle. A prison X-ray taken after his arrest for the murder of Grace Budd revealed that he had a least twenty-nine separate needles in his pelvic region, some of which had eroded over time into fragments.

In January 1917, three years after the birth of their sixth child, Fish's wife left him for a handyman who boarded with them. This rejection seemed to send him on an even faster downward spiral. He started hearing voices. Once he wrapped himself up in a carpet, saying he'd done it on the instructions of John the Apostle.

By his own account Fish committed his first murder in 1910 – a child named Thomas Bedden in Wilmington, Delaware. In 1919 he reportedly mutilated and tortured a mentally retarded boy in New York and killed another in Washington the same year. He admitted killing and eating four-year-old William Gaffney in 1927, and five-year-old Francis McDonal in 1934.

Police suspected Fish was involved in many more murders, though not the 400 he claimed in his initial confession.

At his trial the state was understandably keen for Fish to receive the death penalty, despite his defence of insanity. Fortunately the jury were not convinced by his plea and after listening to his terrifying, not to mention obscene confessions, they found him both sane and guilty of premeditated murder.

CANNIBALS

Fish was sentenced to die in the electric chair and was electrocuted at Sing Sing prison on 16 January 1936. He entered the chamber saying his execution would be 'the supreme thrill of my life – the only one I haven't tried'. Just before the switch was flipped he said, 'I don't even know why I am here.' It took two attempts before he died. The first time the equipment short-circuited due to all the needles that Fish had inserted in his body. The second charge of 3,000 volts fried him.

Seeing execution as the 'supreme thrill' summed Fish up. He'd spent his life pursuing one perversion after another. 'There was no known perversion that he did not practise and practise frequently,' said Dr Frederick Wertham, who made a detailed study of Fish. He listed eighteen sexual perversions that Fish had indulged in, including sado-masochism, exhibitionism, undinism (drinking urine), coprophagia (eating faeces), fetishism and cannibalism. One of his favourite pleasures, Wertham noted, was to soak cotton wool in alcohol, insert it into his anus and set fire to it.

Fish also suffered from religious mania. He was obsessed with the Biblical story of Abraham offering his son Isaac as a sacrifice, and became convinced that he too should sacrifice a young child (even though Abraham didn't actually sacrifice Isaac).

From time to time, Fish would hear the voices of angels uttering strange, archaic-sounding words like 'correcteth', 'delighteth' and 'chastiseth'. He took these as divine commandments to torture and kill.

He used these words to create his own quasi-Biblical

maxims, such as: 'Blessed is the man who correcteth his son in whom he delighteth with stripes [lashings]'; and 'Happy is he that taketh thy little ones and dasheth their heads against stones', the latter being the last line of Psalm 137, *The Rivers of Babylon* (King James Bible).

Even cannibalising his child victims had religious overtones. He told one psychiatrist that interviewed him in prison that he associated eating the flesh and drinking the blood of a child with the 'idea of Holy Communion'.

Unsurprisingly, his favourite passage from the Bible was:

I will make them eat the flesh of their sons and the flesh of their daughters, and they will eat one another's flesh in the siege and in the distress with which their enemies and those who seek their life will distress them.

Jeremiah, 19:9

ED GEIN

Perhaps one of the most notorious of the all-American psychos who also had a taste for human meat was Ed Gein. When police raided his ramshackle farmhouse near Plainfield, Wisconsin, on 16 November 1957, they were shocked to the core by what they found there. They were searching for Bernice Worden, who was missing from her family's hardware store in town – presumed murdered due to blood being found on the floor. They'd come to the right place. Her headless body was hanging in Gein's shed, gutted like a deer carcass.

Moving to the farmhouse itself, police also found part

of the remains of a missing bar owner, which had been turned into a ghoulish mask. She had been missing since 1954. Other body parts were found too, leading investigators to conclude that Gein had robbed graves and possibly killed others.

Gein's home would have made even the Munsters jittery. Using torches and oil lamps to light the rooms, officers found the place hadn't been cleaned in years; piles of rubbish were everywhere and the stench was overpowering. But this was nothing to what else they found in the fallen-down farmhouse.

It was an inventory from Hell, which included: two shin bones, four human noses, a bowl made from half a human skull, ten female heads with the tops sawn off above the eyebrows, bracelets and leggings made from human skin, a shoebox containing nine salted vulvas, a hanging human head, a lampshade made from human skin, a number of shrunken heads, two skulls for Gein's bedposts, a pair of human lips hanging on a string, a full female body suit made from human skin, complete with facial mask and breasts... while Bernice Worden's heart was found in a saucepan on the stove, along with a fridge stuffed full with human internal organs.

The terrifying list went on...

The remains of an estimated fifteen bodies were discovered at Gein's farmhouse. But he couldn't remember how many murders he had committed. What with grave robbing and killing it had become a blur. Police certainly thought there may have been other victims between the years 1954 and 1957, but there was no definitive evidence. Chillingly, neighbours reported to the sheriff that Gein had often brought them gifts of fresh 'venison', yet he had never been hunting or shot a deer in his life.

When he was arrested Gein lived alone on the farm. His father had died in 1940, his brother in 1944 and his mother in 1945. According to a psychological report ordered by the judge at Gein's trial, the deaths took away structure and meaning in his life.

Born in August 1906, Gein had a troubled childhood. His father was a violent drunk; his mother a fanatical Lutheran who taught him that most women were prostitutes and that he should stay away from them.

Unsurprisingly therefore, when living alone at his farmhouse at the age of thirty-nine, he became increasingly uncertain about his masculinity – even considering having his penis amputated. He also thought about having a sex change, which he had read about in newspapers. But the operation was too expensive; and besides it scared him.

At this time he also became interested in the Nazis and the experiments they had carried out on Jews in concentration camps during World War II. It was an unhealthy interest that would explain where he got his ideas for making household furnishings out of human body parts.

When asked why he had committed such terrible atrocities, Gein muttered, 'Well, you see, it was a sex problem. I blame all my trouble on my mother. She should have made me a girl.'

On 16 January 1958 a judge found Gein insane and had him committed to the Central State Hospital at Waupon. Ten years later Gein was considered well enough to stand trial. He was found guilty and declared criminally insane.

CANNIBALS

He was returned to the Central State Hospital, then in 1978 was moved to the Mendota Mental Health Institute. He was considered a model prisoner, always polite and no trouble. He spent his time making rugs and polishing stones. He died of cancer on 26 July 1984, aged seventy-eight.

Twenty-six years earlier – in March 1958 – the people of Plainfield decided to rid the town of Gein's sickening memory and burnt his farmhouse to the ground (when he was told about it, Gein simply said, 'Just as well'). But the townsfolk of Plainfield were unable to stop Gein's legacy from entering the American cultural landscape. In 1960 Alfred Hitchcock's hit movie *Psycho*, based on a book by horror/sci-fi writer Robert Bloch, both horrified and gripped the public imagination. Its main character, the archetypal psycho-killer Norman Bates, was based on Gein and focused on his mother-fixation.

Fourteen years later Tobe Hooper used the idea of a renegade American hunter tracking his (human) prey in *Texas Chainsaw Massacre*, again the cannibal killer 'Leatherface' was loosely based on Gein. Jonathan Demme also backtracked to Gein for background material for his movie *Silence of the Lambs* (1991), this time concentrating on his sexual psychosis.

All this ensured Gein's place in the bogeyman hall of fame. If you wanted your children to behave all you had to do was tell them that, if they didn't, Gein would get them. The only problem was that you could have been tempting fate as there's always another crazed cannibal killer waiting in the wings, ready to reap his own brand of carnage...

ARTHUR SHAWCROSS

Enter Arthur Shawcross. He committed eleven murders between February 1988 and January 1990, and was sentenced to life imprisonment in 1991. The killings all occurred close to the Genesee River, which runs through Rochester, New York. As a result he became known as the 'Genesee River Killer'. All of his victims were women; nine were prostitutes. He either strangled them or killed them with a vicious blow to the head. He would then mutilate their bodies.

When police finally brought him to book they discovered he had served time for murder before. In 1972 he'd been convicted of the rape and manslaughter of eight-year-old Karen Ann Hill in Watertown, upstate New York (while in prison he confessed to murdering another child, a boy, ten-year-old Jack Blake, but wasn't charged).

Shawcross was sentenced to twenty-five years, but got out in fifteen in 1987. Eleven months later, while still on parole, he went on his killing spree in Rochester. Police spent three years hunting the Genesee River Killer, yet didn't check into the sex offender and child killer living locally.

After Shawcross was caught his lengthy confessions painted a sickening picture of how he treated his victims after killing them. He would return to the decomposing bodies, getting sexually excited as he looked at them or mutilated them. He even cut out the vaginas of two of his victims and ate them. He also told shocked investigators how he had cut out Jack Blake's heart and genitals and eaten them.

Shawcross was born on 6 June 1945 to marine corporal Arthur Roy and his teenage bride Bessie. He grew up near Watertown, New York. Considering his repugnant crimes it is tempting to wonder if his childhood was disturbed or not.

130

Shawcross said it was, claiming on numerous occasions that he had been abused as a child. It was criminal psychiatrist Dorothy Otnow Lewis who brought these revelations to light. Besides conducting hours of interviews with Shawcross on behalf of the defence team, she hypnotised him, and reportedly uncovered evidence that his mother had sexually interfered with him when he was a young boy.

The first time Lewis hypnotised Shawcross – regressing him back to childhood – he snapped out of the trance with a start, shaking and sweating with palpable horror. "It was obvious that he was absolutely terrified by something," she told the *Boston Globe* in July 1991. After that, she used a technique that enabled him to remember past events without panicking.

When she hypnotised him a second time, Shawcross revealed that his mother had sodomized him on several occasions when he was a child, making him perform oral sex on her afterwards. Lewis video-taped the session, which was viewed by a reporter from the *Boston Globe* during a seminar given by Lewis. First Lewis asks Shawcross, who had been regressed to age ten, what happened. "She put a stick in there, in my butt," Shawcross replied, crying out: "No, no! I can't breathe... Ohhh..." He then told Lewis that the stick has been pulled out, but that his stomach hurt. "Blood is coming out of my bottom, my fanny," he moaned. "I feel like I'm turned inside out."

In 2006, Shawcross was interviewed by Columbia University forensic psychiatrist Dr. Michael Stone for the Discovery Channel series *Most Evil* – and again insisted he had been sexually abused by his mother.

Rochester psychiatrist, Dr Richard Kraus, however, compiled an extensive report on Shawcross for the murder trial and concluded that, far from being abused, he'd had a happy and caring childhood.

Shawcross also tried to pin the blame for the murders he'd committed on his time fighting in the Vietnam War.

'I was trained to kill,' he said. 'I was not trained to stop. Even today that bothers me.'

Shawcross claimed he regularly went on lone search and destroy missions, where he had licence to wipe out everything. In one incident Shawcross surprised two Vietcong women in the jungle. He killed the first woman and tied the second to a tree. He then made her watch as he cut up, cooked and ate her dead comrade:

I made a little campfire there, and I took the leg, the right leg from that woman's body, from the knee to the hip, took the skin off, took the cords out and took the fat off and it was only – what? – dead leg around anyway. And I had crushed rock salt in one of my oil pouches, and I sprinkled water on it, and I'm staring at this other girl because I don't know if she speaks English or whatever, broken English, and I'm putting the rock salt on it, and I'm sitting there cooking over a fire, you know. And when I bit into it, looking at... staring this other girl in the eye, she just urinated right there, you know.

When psychiatrist Richard Kraus went through Shawcross's medical history, he found that the psychiatrists who had treated him all gave up in the end: all they could do was dismiss him as 'different', 'odd' or just 'untreatable'. He appeared to be some kind of medical aberration. Unlike many killers, cannibal or otherwise, his childhood, so far as doctors could tell, had been unremarkable. They had little to go on as to what may have motivated Shawcross to commit his terrible crimes.

What nobody looked at – or if they did they knew better than to delve too deeply into it – was a programme set up by the US Central Intelligence Agency (CIA) called MK-ULTRA. It ran for twenty-five years (possibly longer) and conducted psychological experiments on both volunteers and unwitting subjects – at home and abroad – to find the key to the unconscious mind, memory and volition. The goal was to create the perfect assassin and to protect America from the programmed assassins of other countries.

All records of this almost science fiction-like project were destroyed in 1973 on the orders of CIA director Richard Helms. He claimed that MK-ULTRA had not come up with anything worthwhile, which was why the project had been wound up. The question is, if the project was so unsuccessful, why were the documents shredded?

As it is, we don't know who the test subjects were, or what was done to them. We don't know how they were programmed (if they were). Nor do we know what they might do, or what they might have done...

What is known is that some people who went on to become murderers and serial killers spent time at institutions receiving CIA/MK-ULTRA funding for 'special testing' – people like Charles Manson and 'Cinque', the leader of the Symbionese Liberation Army that kidnapped heiress Patty Hearst.

Given what is known, it could well be that Arthur Shawcross was another example of someone whose mind had been tampered with by MK-ULTRA. It would certainly explain why he was sent out on lone search and destroy missions in Vietnam and why, as he later boasted, he relished the atrocities he committed.

Most suggestive is the fact that Shawcross is thought to have served as a Phoenix operative during the Vietnam War. According to Douglas Valentine, in his book *The Phoenix Program* (Morrow 1990), the Phoenix teams consisted of navy SEALs working with CTs (Counter Terrorists) described by one participant as 'a combination of ARVN [Army of the Republic of Vietnam] deserters, VC turncoats, and bad motherfucker criminals the South Vietnamese couldn't deal with in prison, so they turned them over to us.'

The CIA spooks were happy to employ the services of these men who 'taught [their] SEAL comrades the secrets of the psy war campaign'. So depraved were these agency recruits that some of them 'would actually devour their enemies' vital organs'.

Unsurprisingly, when Shawcross returned home, he couldn't switch off. If indeed he had been programmed to kill, no one got around to reprogramming him to be a non-homicidal citizen.

One other curious element in the Arthur Shawcross story is that, during his first prison term in the 1970s, he talked of being possessed by a thirteenth-century cannibal called 'Ariemes'. He felt this was what drove him to rape, murder and commit acts of cannibalism. He also spoke in the voice of Ariemes when under hypnosis.

Could the concept of Ariemes have been planted in Shawcross's mind by operatives from the MK-ULTRA programme using brainwashing techniques?

If so, his penchant for cannibalism was a government creation.

SIX:
MOTHER RUSSIA

ANDREI CHIKATILO

In the days of the former Soviet Union such things as unemployment, homosexuality or prostitution did not exist. Nor were there any serial killers. All these were strictly the preserve of the decadent, capitalist West. That was the official line, at least.

The reality, of course, was very different. In fact the worst serial killer the world has ever known – who also had cannibal tendencies – operated in the Soviet Union between 1978 and 1990. This was Andrei Chikatilo, who admitted to killing fifty-three people during his twelve-year murder spree. The majority of his victims were killed around Rostov-on-Don, a city made up of drab Soviet-era tower blocks and crumbling historic buildings.

When police finally caught Chikatilo the horrific details of his crimes – which were unbelievably sadistic – stunned the world, when they came out during his long and harrowing trial.

Chikatilo was born in 1936 in Yablochnoye, a little village

in the Ukraine. Like the rest of the people who lived in the region, his family were still suffering from the famine that had been artificially induced by Stalin in 1932–1933 to force private farmers into collectives. They could recall how, at its peak, the famine had forced starving villagers to resort to cannibalism, eating relatives who had died.

There were also rumours that roving bands of cannibals had kidnapped children, killed them and sold their meat at local markets. Whether this was true or not is hard to tell. What is certain is Chikatilo's mother told him that his older brother Stephan had been abducted and killed by one of these gangs. Not surprisingly, this scared the hell out of Chikatilo, giving him terrifying nightmares about cannibalism from an early age.

Chikatilo's family were very poor, continually struggling to find enough money to live. Because of their poverty they were forced to sleep together on a large wooden platform, which served as a bed. Unfortunately Chikatilo was a bedwetter, so the rest of the family were affected too. His mother Anna, who was hot-tempered and domineering, would regularly fly into wild rages at her son about this.

By the time he reached puberty the condition stopped. Unluckily for him it was replaced by an equally embarrassing condition – extremely premature ejaculation. He would often have an orgasm before his penis had become fully erect. This led to traumatic situations with girls, who often taunted him for his lack of control.

When he was sixteen, Chikatilo started to show signs of pathology. In one incident a friend of his younger sister's visited his family's home. He was the only one in. She was only about ten or eleven, but Chikatilo felt a sudden overwhelming urge to rape her. He grabbed her and threw her to the ground. In the struggle he ejaculated, which was fortunate for the girl as it saved her from being raped.

Chikatilo went on to study at university and became a teacher at a local school. Despite his sexual problems he married a miner's daughter called Feodosia in 1963. Feodosia didn't see premature ejaculation as a big deal. As far as she was concerned, she could have done a lot worse than Chikalito. He didn't smoke or drink, nor was he boastful or conceited. They even managed to have two children – Ludmilla in 1965 and Yuri in 1969. Chikatilo's ejaculation problem hadn't been miraculously cured; he impregnated Feodosia by coming on her stomach, then directing the semen inside her with his fingers.

Chikatilo worked hard at his teaching job and was kind to Feodosa and their two children. Other people's children, however, were a different matter; he was caught molesting some of his female pupils, apparently getting a kick out of the way they screamed and pushed him away when he grabbed them. Incredibly, no action was taken against Chikatilo. In 1978 he was simply transferred to a less sensitive teaching post at a mining school in Shakhty. The incident was brushed under the carpet; even Feodosia had no idea about what her husband had been up to.

Although a family flat went with his new job, Chikatilo secretly bought a ramshackle shack on the other side of town. No one knew about this until police captured him twelve years later. He took prostitutes there, then runaway teenagers and finally little girls.

At first he may simply have used the shack to try and overcome his ejaculation problems. But it turned out that only terrible, bestial acts could bring him true sexual satisfaction.

He first discovered this in December 1978 when he lured nine-year-old Lena Zakotnova to his shack. He'd met her at a tram stop and had struck up a conversation, his fatherly manner putting her at her ease. She told him she was desperate for the toilet. He said, 'I live nearby, you're welcome to use mine.' She said, 'Thank you,' and went with him.

When they arrived at the shack, he turned on the lights, closed the door behind them, then leapt on her. 'The girl was frightened and cried out,' he recalled in his confession twelve years later. 'I couldn't get an erection and I couldn't get my penis into her vagina.'

But the need to have an orgasm overwhelmed him and he decided he would do it by any means possible.

'Her cries excited me further,' he said. 'Lying on her and moving in imitation of the sex act, I pulled out my knife and started to stab her. I climaxed, as if it had happened during a natural sex act. I started to put the sperm into her vagina by hand.'

By chance Chikatilo, now forty-two, had discovered he could achieve normal orgasm through abnormal means – by violence and killing.

He was almost caught for the murder. Lena's body was recovered from the river, and people had seen him with her. Chikatilo's wife, however, gave him an alibi, insisting he had been with her at home all evening.

Police then pulled in a man named Kravchenko, who had a record of similar crimes and lived just around the corner from where the body had been dumped. Kravchenko was executed in 1983, protesting his innocence to the end.

After Chikatilo's first killing there was no going back. He

found himself obsessed with the need to repeat what he had done to Lena. He resisted at first – to the point that he would cut short business trips if the temptation to find another victim came upon him.

But in autumn 1981 his terrible desires overcame him. He was on business in Novoshakhtinsk and spotted a runaway girl, seventeen-year-old Larisa Tkachenko, sitting in a bus shelter. He went up to her and struck up a conversation, which resulted in the teenager offering to have sex with him for a little money. Chikatilo led her into a nearby woods, leapt on her and wrestled her to the ground. In a frenzy of violence he strangled her to near-unconsciousness, then sank his teeth into her neck, drinking the blood and smearing it over his face.

Finally, he bit off her nipples and swallowed them, then mutilated her genitals. This killing brought him another new discovery: eating the flesh and drinking the blood of his victims also brought him to orgasm.

There was no holding Chikatilo back now. He got down to killing on a regular basis.

He also decided to give up teaching and took a post as a supplies administrator for an industrial firm called Rostovnerud. His career change also had more sinister motives. The job involved travelling all over the Soviet Union, sourcing supplies and collecting replacement parts, making it an ideal cover for finding new victims.

What's more, Chikatilo was good at talking to strangers, and had a knack for getting children to trust him. 'He had an amazing talent for it,' said one of the investigating officers later. 'He could join a bus queue and say to the person in front: "Hey, where did you buy those beautiful mushrooms?" and before you knew it he would have the whole crowd chatting.'

At his trial, Chikatilo was asked why he thought children went with him. 'I must have had a kind of magnetism,' he answered.

Almost all the people he killed were runaways or homeless. In his confessions, after he was captured, Chikatilo described them as 'déclassé elements'. In other words, he saw them as underclass and not worthy of being alive; people you could use without guilt or remorse to satisfy your own sadistic pleasures. '[They were] always pestering people for one thing or another,' he said. 'They beg, demand and seize things... they crawl into your very soul, demanding money, food, vodka and offering themselves for sex.' Obviously, ridding the streets of what he saw as 'vermin' wasn't his main motive; but perhaps it was his way of justifying the terrible deeds he had perpetrated.

In the end, however, frenzied attacks began to feel routine – Chikatilo wanted to spice up his activities to recapture the vibrancy of his first sexual killings. He did this by using his knife with more precision when he stabbed his victims – inflicting shallower wounds to prolong suffering and heighten his enjoyment. He also took to slicing off boys' genitals and the uterus from female victims, which he ate to attain even greater sexual pleasure.

Chikatilo's wife later told police that he carried cooking utensils with him on business/killing trips. And police found the remnants of campfires near some of the victims, all of which suggested that he also cooked up his victims' sex organs.

CANNIBALS

During summer 1984 Chikatilo killed ten people in two months – more than one a week. Clearly a beast was on the loose. Something had to be done. So in 1985 a team from the Soviet Union's Department for Crimes of Special Importance was sent to investigate. They were incredibly thorough and over a number of years cleared up ninety-five unsolved murders. Chikatilo's, however, were not among them. And the killings continued, particularly around the Rostov-on-Don region.

The police ended up saturating the area with undercover cops. Then finally, in November 1990, a breakthrough came. Chikatilo was stopped and questioned when a police officer spotted him coming out of some woods, stopping to wash his hands and shoes at a water fountain. Police searched the woods and found another body. After Chikatilo's semen was tested and proved a match with that found on the body, he was charged with thirty-six murders – promptly confessing to another nineteen.

For the next eighteen months investigators questioned him about every one of his crimes. He was also sent to the Serbsky Psychiatric Institute in Moscow, where he was examined for two months. Psychiatrists noted that Chikatilo discussed the murders 'calmly and coldly' and that he wasn't deranged enough to be unaware that he was doing wrong.

The subsequent reports described him as a sadist who was cautious in the extreme when carrying out his premeditated murders. It was noted that he tended not to kill during the winter months, presumably because it was too cold. The point was he *thought* about what he was doing, down to the last detail. Therefore psychiatrists declared him legally sane.

A key part of any Russian criminal investigation involves

a procedure known as the 'experiment'. The accused is asked to act out exactly how the crime was committed in front of a camera. Chikatilo was no exception. Using a tailor's dummy he showed watching investigators how he killed each person – including his first victim Lena. Incredibly, displaying no remorse whatsoever, he chatted and joked as he re-enacted the death scenes.

His wife, Feodosia, was shocked to the core. She couldn't believe Chikatilo was capable of the terrible things the police said he had done. After all, hadn't he always been a devoted father who loved his children? 'I could never imagine him being able to murder one person, let alone more than fifty,' she said.

When she finally accepted the truth she blamed herself for not suspecting something was wrong – and for not inquiring into all those business trips he took. If she had, some of the killings might have been prevented.

Chikatilo finally came to trial on 14 April 1992 in Rostov-on-Don's main court. The proceedings lasted six months and Chikatilo had to be kept in a cage – not to keep him in, but to keep the relatives and friends of his victims from tearing him apart. You couldn't blame them; he had committed the vilest crimes imaginable not just against grown women, but against boys aged between eight and sixteen, and girls aged between nine and seventeen.

The sheer horror of his activities stunned the court. Relatives – and even tough prison guards – fainted when they heard how Chikatilo had boiled and eaten sawn-off testicles and nipples from his victims, and how many of them had still been alive when the butchering began.

It was even revealed that Chikatilo had carved slits in some corpses so he could practise his own brand of necrophiliac sex.

In a bid to feign insanity and escape a death sentence, Chikatilo often acted as if he had lost his mind. From the safety of his cage he exposed his penis, sang the communist anthem, 'The Internationale', and at one point tore of his shirt and shouted, 'It's time for me to give birth!'

It was to no avail. On 15 October 1992 the presiding judge found Chikatilo guilty and sane on all but one of the fifty-three murder charges.

He was sent to a Moscow prison to await execution, which was done quickly and without ceremony in the Russian style. On 16 February 1994, early in the morning, two soldiers arrived unannounced at Chikatilo's cell and led him down to the execution room. One of them put a pistol to the back of his head and killed him with a single shot.

Strangely, but in common with numerous other cannibal killers, Chikatilo is on record as saying that he believed something outside himself made him commit his terrible acts. 'The more I've thought about it, the more I've come to the conclusion that I suffer from some kind of sickness,' he told investigators at one point. 'It was as if something directed me, something outside me, when I committed these murders.'

Clearly, this could have been another ruse to make it appear like he was insane. Or it could have been a very real feeling he had. Perhaps his sadistic urges lurked deep in his unconscious mind and, when they came to the surface, it felt as if another being had taken over – something alien.

Psychologists, particularly if they are of a Freudian or Jungian bent, will accept this as plausible. But they won't accept the idea that an actual entity is involved.

Nor would I, most of the time... But the fact is, a very large percentage of the world does believe in gods and spirits and would not have a problem with Chikatilo's claim that something 'outside' was directing him.

Before we discuss Chikatilo any further, let's look at how other cultures treat the idea of spirit possession, taking French writer Serge Bramly's experiences as a starting point. He witnessed many spirit possession ceremonies in Brazil while researching his book *Macumba* (City Lights 1994). One ceremony in particular brought it home to him that gods, spirits and other beings may not simply be 'all in the mind'.

As Bramly sat down to watch, the master of ceremonies raised his arms to the sky and cried out to the spirits of Macumba, 'I greet the ways of Umbanda... Xango and Oxala!'

This prayer to the gods was the first stage of a ritual held before a large congregation of devotees to the Brazilian religion of Macumba, which has roots in Africa and is related to Haitian Voodoo and Cuban Santeria. When the prayer was over everyone applauded and the ceremonial drums began to pound hypnotically.

The MC, a middle-aged man with a greying moustache, then launched into a series of calls, intended to attract the gods down to earth. As he did this, intricate symbols representing the gods of Macumba (known as Orixas) were traced on the floor. Finally a candle was placed inside each one.

In the centre of the large room, staring into space, stood

Maria Jose, the temple priestess, known as the mother of the gods. She was a stately middle-aged black woman who ran the proceedings. After a while, a group of dancers, mainly women, surrounded her.

They moved gracefully to the beat of the drums and bowed each time they passed the sacred symbols on the floor.

Suddenly, one of them let out a sharp cry and threw herself onto one of the symbols on the floor, writhing and moaning in ecstasy. Another dancer lit a pipe, then doubled over, resting her weight on a cane. When she spoke she had the voice of an old man.

A male dancer suddenly threw his head back, laughed maniacally and gesticulated like a disjointed puppet. Then a large black woman lit a thick cigar, puffed heavily on it, and slugged back a whole bottle of cachaca – fifty-per-cent-proof sugar-cane liquor.

All of them were possessed by various gods from the Macumba pantheon.

Given life by the mediums, the 'gods' hugged each other and sat down on the floor to minister to their devotees – some of whom had come to receive healing, improve their luck or simply for advice.

Eventually, when all those seeking help had been seen to, the ceremony wound down. The gods then left the mediums and they returned to their normal selves.

Much of Bramly's book *Macumba* consists of interviews with the priestess Maria Jose. In one of the talks she explained that the gods mount the mediums much as a rider would mount a horse. 'At that moment', she said, 'the head of the medium exists only as a vessel, a simple vase offered to the god. The medium has no will, no memory, no personality. The god enters the medium and makes herself or himself at home. It's the god you see and hear. Once the god is gone the medium can't remember anything that happened during the trance.'

When asked why it was necessary for the mediums – particularly the women – to drink huge amounts of strong alcohol and smoke big, black cigars, Maria Jose replied, 'When they drink and smoke, the daughters of the gods are no longer themselves. It is the gods who are drinking and smoking.'

Once the ceremony was over, she told Bramly, the mediums are 'no more drunk than you or I'.

She also stressed that devotees of Macumba see possession as being of great benefit to the community; they don't see it as a dark and evil occurrence as we might in the West. 'The mediums lend their bodies to the gods in order for them to become incarnate; so that they can be with us, speak to us, answer our questions, give us strength,' she said. 'It's a kind of exchange. We give life to the gods, and they in return agree to help us.'

But spiritist religions like Macumba and Voodoo do accept that there are also dark spirits that can wreak havoc on the world through the humans they possess. These clearly have to be exorcised by a priest or priestess of the religion.

I personally witnessed a spirit exorcism a couple of years back in Harlesden, north-west London, while researching a story for a magazine article. It was midday and the sun was beating down on row after row of late nineteenth-/early twentieth-century terraces and red brick blocks of flats.

146

Inside one flat, Edmond Labady, a self-styled Voodoo priest dressed in flowing white robes, was beating out a hypnotic rhythm on a small drum.

The room was completely blacked out. On a table to the side of the room were dozens of candles, along with dried beans, beads and a bottle of holy water, all laid out symbolically for the coming ritual.

A six-year-old child was dragged kicking and screaming into the room by his parents. They believed he was possessed by an evil spirit, and they had hired Labady – who was well known among the local Afro-Caribbean, Brazilian and African community as an exorcist – to remove the entity from the child.

After Labady dabbed spiritual oil on the youngster's forehead, the parents started chanting prayers to the Voodoo gods, petitioning them to make the evil spirit leave. Within minutes their eyes begin to look glazed – a tell-tale sign that they'd entered the kind of hypnotic trance states found in Haitian Voodoo – and Brazilian Macumba.

The child was shaking and screaming so violently that Labady was forced to restrain him. The witchdoctor sent out 'energy vibrations' to the child, which he believed would put him in direct psychic communication with the child.

Labady then let out an almighty yell, 'A good spirit is calling for the bad spirit to leave! Demon! Get out of this poor child!'

After a cacophony of cries and moans from the parents – and more shouted incantations from Labady – the child suddenly went quiet and stopped shaking completely. He was relaxed and calm. The evil spirit had vanished.

Rituals like this are becoming increasingly common in

Britain's towns and cities. They are usually performed underground and out of the prying gaze of the general public. With good reason. Most of us would consider such rites to be tantamount to child cruelty, if not plain satanic. Not for one minute would we take the notion of evil spirits seriously; nor would we consider such ceremonies as a type of holistic medicine. Yet as far as Labady is concerned – and the scores of others who practise African witchcraft, or Juju, in Britain – such work brings tangible benefits both to children and the community as a whole.

'I'm not doing anything wrong – I'm helping people,' insisted the old man, who was originally from West Africa. 'There have never been any problems. If the child is not exorcised then it will grow up to be horrible – I get results.'

He rejected the notion that the exorcisms could inflict long-term psychological damage on the children. On the contrary: 'By making the evil spirits leave them, the children will not drift into crime, drugs or violence,' he said. 'Once they get older they are OK. Parents never come back to see me.'

Had Labady – or, indeed, Maria Jose – been confronted with Chikatilo they'd likely have considered him to have been possessed by a nefarious entity. His claim that something 'outside' directed his actions would have made perfect sense to them.

In fact, I related Chikatilo's story to Labady. In his opinion there was no doubt that Chikatilo was possessed by a bad spirit. 'Let me be clear,' he added, 'the bad spirit wasn't an excuse for the evil he did. He had to die, there wasn't a choice.'

As far as Labady was concerned, it had been too late; Chikatilo needed to have been exorcised when he was young.

'Bad spirit would've entered him when he was a child,' he explained. 'If he'd been exorcised by somebody with power, the killings might have been prevented.'

Labady said he would have exorcised Chikatilo before he was executed, 'So he could know peace and go to God cleansed.'

As for the relatives of Chikatilo's victims, Labady said, 'We need to pray for them, they had their little ones taken from them by a terrible force that should not have been let into this world.'

SASCHA SPESIVTSEV

Unsurprisingly, the idea of exorcism very much appealed to my cannibal correspondent Eric Soames. It fitted his belief that he was possessed – and that a 'bad spirit' was behind his pathological desire to eat human flesh. When I spoke to him about exorcism he asked me to arrange one for him. He felt it was worth a try as conventional psychological treatments hadn't worked. I agreed and asked my Canadian shaman friend, Dr Crazywolf, to do it. But we'll come to that at the end of this book.

In the meantime, let's briefly return to Russia to look at how, in the aftermath of the Chikatilo murders and the collapse of the Soviet Union in 1991, a spate of cannibal killings swept through the country. It echoed the early years of Soviet Russia when, due to food shortages, roving gangs of cannibals were said to be kidnapping children.

Newspaper reports across the former Soviet Union spoke of cases of vagrants being eaten, or their bodies being cut up and sold to unsuspecting passers-by. One criminologist was quoted as saying, 'We have information about cases where human flesh is sold in street markets; also when homeless people kill each other and sell the flesh. Every month we find corpses with missing body parts.'

He wasn't exaggerating.

In 1996 alone ten people were charged with killing and eating fellow humans, and police estimated that at least thirty people were eaten that year.

One notorious case involved thirty-seven-year-old Ilshat Kuzikov. He murdered three people who made the mistake of visiting him. He marinated cuts of their flesh with onions and put the grisly concoction in a bag, which he left outside to keep cool. Kuzikov used Pepsi bottles to store their blood and hung several ears on the wall for snacks.

When police raided his home he offered them some meat and vodka if they would turn a blind eye to what he'd done. He said he had resorted to cannibalism because he couldn't afford to eat properly on his twenty-dollars-a-month income.

Also in 1996, police in Sevastopol, a port city in the Ukraine, were called in to investigate a murder. Nothing prepared them for the carnage they discovered when they entered the home of a former convict and found the butchered remains of human bodies that had been prepared for eating. Three people had been stabbed to death and mutilated by the thirty-three-year-old suspect. In the kitchen, investigators found the internal organs of two victims in saucepans, and nearby on a plate was a freshly roasted piece of human flesh.

Then, during the winter of 1996/7, thirty-eight-year-old Vladimir Nikolayev was arrested for eating people in the town of Novocheboksary. A known criminal, police had called at his home on an unrelated matter, but were shocked to find roasted human meat on his stove. Other body parts were found frozen in the snow on Nikolayev's balcony.

Worse still was the case of twenty-seven-year-old Sascha Spesivtsev, which came to light by accident in 1996. Spesivtsev shared a flat with his mother Ludmilla and their beloved Doberman dog in the Siberian town of Novokuznetsk. Unfortunately, Sascha had a sadistic nature and used to beat and abuse his mother mercilessly.

Oddly, considering the severely dysfunctional nature of the family, Spesivtsev's sister had managed to forge a very successful career, as secretary to a well-known judge in the region.

It was by accident that Spesivtsev was exposed as a deranged cannibal killer. Neighbours had called in a plumber to fix a broken water pipe. He needed access to Spesivtsev's apartment to stem the leak. When no one answered the door, he was forced to break in. He stood there in horror. It was a human abattoir; blood was splattered all over the walls. In the kitchen were lots of bowls filled with human body parts, and a mutilated girl with her head missing was found in the bath. Another girl, still alive but seriously wounded, was on the sofa in the lounge.

The plumber called the emergency services and police and medics arrived within minutes.

The wounded girl told the public prosecutor what had happened. Apparently, Spesivtsev's mother had lured her, along with two others to the flat. Spesivtsev promptly beat them and raped them. He then killed one of the girls and forced the other two to cut her up in the bath. After that,

Spesivtsev's mother cooked up the body parts for dinner. The second dead girl had been killed by Spesivtsev's Doberman, which bit through her throat.

Seventeen hours after giving her statement, the girl died of her injuries.

The police found a diary in the flat which detailed the murders of nineteen girls. Spesivtsev was suspected of having been responsible for over a dozen other deaths, but these weren't investigated due to lack of funds.

Spesivtsev, however, was still at large. He'd escaped over the balcony when he heard the plumber breaking down the door. He was later caught as he attempted to rape a young girl.

At the close of his trial Spesivtsev was found guilty of nineteen murders and sentenced to death. He was later declared insane and put into a special psychiatric hospital; Ludmilla Spesivtseva denied any involvement, but was convicted as an accomplice and sentenced to life in prison.

The killing continues. On July 15 2002, police in the central Ukrainian town of Zhytomyr said they had arrested three men and a woman on suspicion of murdering and cannibalising up to six people, including an eighteen-year-old girl. 'They killed a young woman in a forest and then cut out fleshy parts of the body and ate them. This is horrible,' a police spokeswoman told the Reuters news agency.

The girl was scalped and decapitated, then her head was boiled in water and eaten by the killers. The cannibal gang was arrested several days after the murder when they went to meet the girl's parents to collect a $3,000 ransom.

SEVEN:
HISTORICAL
BLOOD LUST

SAWNEY BEANE

Tribal cannibalism – which generally has a spiritual not psychopathic motive – dates back to ancient times. Archaeologists found that the diet of 500,000-year-old Peking Man, unearthed in China in the 1920s, included human flesh. Evidence suggestive of cannibalism has been found in many caves and rock shelters lived in by Neanderthal Man. And Cro-Magnon Man, the first to be termed Homo Sapiens ('thinking man'), is also thought to have eaten his fellow man, at least on occasion.

The Aztecs, of course, practised ritual sacrifice – which often included cannibalism – on a massive scale. In the fifteenth century the Aztec's eighth emperor, Ahuitzotl, ordered the sacrifice of eighty thousand prisoners to dedicate a temple to the gods. The massacre took four days of non-stop killing and the gutters ran red with blood. The priests flayed the corpses and lubricated their own naked bodies with their fat before pulling on the skin like a wet suit. The slaughterers and their families followed this up with a cannibal feast.

Colin Wilson – the true crime writer and ancient mysteries expert – however, is sceptical that any spiritual motive was involved in this. 'To say all this was done in a spirit of religious piety is obviously absurd,' he says in *Atlantis and the Kingdom of the Neanderthals* (2006). 'Any criminologist knows that sadistic murder becomes an addiction.'

This was certainly true in the case of Sawney Beane, whose band of cannibals terrorised the Galloway area of Scotland during the Middle Ages. His cannibalism began as a way to survive out in the wilds, then seemed to turn into a compulsion.

Scotland was an unruly and often lawless place at that time. You couldn't blame the Scots. Life was hard and they had a lot to contend with during this time. Not only did they have to face cold, bleak winters and all too regular crop failure, but the English were forever trying to crush them and bring the country under their control. Soldiers were regularly sent on sorties to burn farms and villages, making people homeless and thus unable to rebel.

All this resulted in an unstable society in which theft, violence and often murder were commonplace. But most people – despite the chronic food shortages – would not resort to eating their own kind. All except Sawney Beane, that is, whose name went on to become synonymous with cannibalism.

A number of sources – dating from the late sixteenth to the mid-nineteenth centuries – provide the details of Beane's reign of terror. But the most popular and reliable version of his story is found in John Nicholson's *Historical and Traditional Tales Connected with the South of Scotland* (1834).

Some historians today, however, doubt that Sawney Beane ever existed. Ronald Holmes, writing in *The Legend of Sawney Beane* (1975), for example, says he was nothing more than a legend – 'a primeval presence from the dark past of the human mind'.

But the various sources are compelling, leading many experts to conclude that a cannibal – possibly with a different name – really was on the loose for more than two decades in Scotland during the Middle Ages.

Sawney Beane, if that really was his name, was born in East Lothian, nine miles east of Edinburgh, some time between 1385 and 1390. His parents named him Alexander after his father. But because of his thatch of blazing red hair he was dubbed 'Sawney', the old Scottish term for Sandy.

Sawney's father was a hardworking peasant who eked out a living as a hedge layer and ditch digger. Sawney, on the other hand, was prone to idleness. He also had a wild streak and his behaviour was often dangerously violent. He eventually took up with a girl whose temperament was, as chronicler John Nicholson put it, 'as viciously inclined as himself'. It was a match made in hell. Together they ran riot. They were always brawling and stealing. Not surprisingly, they weren't exactly popular with their neighbours, and were always in trouble with the authorities.

In the end, Sawney's parents had little choice but to throw him out. He was now in his late teens so as far as they were concerned he would be able to look after himself.

Sawney and his girlfriend hung around the area for a

while. But villagers got sick of their continual trouble-making and drove them out, warning them never to come back.

They kept up their criminal and violent ways and were likely declared outlaws by the King's local agent. Now on the run, they were often only days or hours away from capture.

Eventually they came to Galloway, now in South Ayrshire, on the south-west coast of Scotland. It was lonely and desolate. But the windswept dunes and rugged coastline offered dozens of hiding places, making it an ideal base for evading the law.

They hid by day, but ventured out during the evenings and early mornings to prey on unsuspecting travellers on the lonely tracks connecting the isolated villagers along the coast. In those days travelling from place to place was hazardous – you were always fare game for robbers and highwaymen. Disappearances were far more common than they are today.

Eventually, they found an even better base – a cave located halfway between the tiny villages of Lendalfoot and Ballantrae, and close to an outcrop of land called Bennane Head. The cave was situated at the foot of a steep cliff. It then wound and weaved for nearly a mile inside Bennane Head, finally leading off into a maze of dead ends. When the tide came in, the waves surged some 200 yards into the cave's mouth.

It was the ultimate hideout. No one in their wildest dreams would suspect that anyone lived there.

But the Beanes (Sawney's girlfriend was now as good as his wife) were not just anyone. They were about to transform from violent petty thieves into monstrous bloodthirsty ghouls, prowling the rugged landscape for victims.

This grisly transformation wasn't born of a sadistic or psychotic streak, however. On the contrary, it was down to good sense. To survive on the fringes of society as outlaws was no easy matter; food was the biggest issue. They could hardly expect to get away with robbing and killing unwary travellers, then take their plunder to villages to sell or barter for provisions. That would have been a sure recipe for their undoing.

Another alternative would have been cattle rustling. But that was too risky. And besides, it was a hanging offence.

In the end, the solution was staring them in the face; rather than just kill and rob their victims, they would eat them too. After all, a dead human is not much different to a dead animal. Both offer good cuts of meat. But the advantage of hunting humans over small animals is the average human carcass will provide around sixty pounds of edible meat. Therefore the Beanes could have survived on a single kill for a month or more. Obviously the meat would need to be preserved. But Sawney's wife had the answer: she rubbed the various cuts of meat with salt from the tidal basin or soaked them in brine, other sections were smoked over fires.

With a good solid base and steady flow of food the Beanes soon set about starting a family. In total they had fourteen children. Eventually the children bred amongst themselves (incest being the only option), and Sawney and his wife found themselves with eighteen grandsons and fourteen granddaughters.

They were a terrifying tribe of cannibals. The children, of course, would have considered the hunting of humans for food as normal. If you'd taken one of them to a city like Edinburgh, they'd have viewed the people going about their business the same way as a lion eyeing up its prey.

Not surprisingly the populace around Lendalfoot and Ballantrae started to get worried. A lot of people were disappearing. Recognising that this could lead to their undoing, the Beanes simply opened up their hunting grounds and went further afield for their prey. They would lay in wait around Galloway, ambushing travellers as they passed by.

Although they behaved like blood-thirsty wild beasts, the Beanes employed almost military strategy when hunting their human prey. Some of their band would be sent ahead as scouts to make sure no one else was on the road behind their intended targets. They were well aware that being surprised by 'have-a-go-heroes' would likely be their undoing. They also knew they needed time to cover their tracks and haul the carcasses of their victims back to their lair.

They got away with this for more than two decades, leaving the populace in mortal terror. Fewer and fewer people travelled the lonely roads. Businesses that relied on outside trade began to collapse. Many people moved away.

Disappearances were reported to the King's magistrates. This led to soldiers being sent in to investigate. Sometimes they made arrests and people were hanged if they couldn't provide a good reason for being out in the wilds. Increasingly paranoid locals occasionally took the law into their own hands and conducted lynchings.

Innkeepers also fell under suspicion. The reasoning was, if a traveller stayed overnight at an inn before disappearing then a disreputable innkeeper could well have followed them and killed them for their money and belongings. So a number of innkeepers were sent to the gallows.

It was all in vain. The disappearances continued.

The Beanes, however, gave the game away when they became so inundated with human meat that they started disposing of the unusable parts in the sea. Unsurprisingly, some of it got washed ashore when the tide came in.

Locals immediately realised that whoever was responsible for the disappearances was not a mere robber and murderer. The remains that had washed ashore had teeth and knife marks on them, forcing people to conclude that a tribe of cannibals had been operating along the coast all those years.

Although highly meticulous in their actions, the Beanes finally came unstuck in spring or summer 1435. They ambushed a young couple returning along the coast road from a village fair some distance away. They shared a horse, the man at the front, the woman behind with her hands around his waist. As they approached the ambush point, the Beanes leapt out at them. Screaming and yelling, they dragged the woman from the horse, quickly slitting her throat. Some of the feral band lapped at the blood as it spurted from the wound. Others sliced open her belly and pulled out her entrails as if they were field dressing a dead animal.

The husband managed to stay on the horse. He drew his sword and attempted to fend off the rabid attackers. Slashing right then left, it looked like a useless battle. There were too many of them – all coming at him like wolves. Just then a group of about twenty others, who had also been to the village fair, arrived and helped drive the Beanes off.

Terrified and shocked, the husband babbled out the incredible tale of what had happened to his wife, whose ripped and torn remains lay on the road in a pool of blood.

They escorted the grief-stricken man back to Glasgow, where he told the story to local magistrates (the validity of the tale was backed up by his companions). Word was sent to the King, James I of Scotland, at Edinburgh. He immediately assembled four hundred soldiers and led them himself to the location of the attack. They spent days with a pack of tracker dogs scouring the roads and lanes between Lendalfoot and Ballantrae, but drew a blank.

Finally, as they were riding along the beach below Bennane Head cliff, the dogs made a dash for the narrow opening in the rock face, and stood there barking and howling. Because the sea ran a good way into the cave opening, they couldn't see how anyone could be in there, and nearly left. But to be certain, King James and some of the men lit some torches and went in to investigate. They wandered along the twists and turns of the cave, peering into one dark hole after another. Eventually they came upon a chamber that stank of death, and was piled high with human bones. Some were clearly old; others were fresh and still had flesh clinging to them.

They immediately sent a runner back to fetch the rest of the men – all armed to the teeth – so they could search every inch of the cavern.

They found chambers full of half-rotted clothes, swords, purses of money and other valuables – and, of course, endless piles of human arms, legs and other body parts. It was like a slaughterhouse.

They went deeper and deeper into the dark, dank cave until eventually they found the Beanes, who shrieked and growled like trapped animals. After a furious fight the soldiers managed to overpower the twenty-seven savage men and twenty-one women. They then bound them in chains and took them back to Edinburgh.

The human remains in the cave were carefully removed and given a Christian burial.

News of the captured cannibal band shot around Scotland. People were literally baying for their blood. After spending just one night in Edinburgh's Tollbooth jail, the Beanes were taken to Leith (now the site of Edinburgh's Leith docks). There – with the women forced to watch – the men had their arms and legs chopped off with axes and were left to bleed to death. The women were then chained in groups to three huge stakes and burnt alive, much as suspected witches were. To the very end, the Beanes refused to show remorse for their crimes and died shrieking curses at their captors.

It is not known how many people fell victim to the Beanes over the twenty-five years they roamed the lonely Galloway landscape. But the various accounts tend to agree it was around the one thousand mark. Considering the number of mouths to feed, and the length of time they were operating, this could well have been the case.

SEYE THE BANDIT

A few hundred years later, across the English Channel in France, another terrifying hunter of humans prowled on the lonely and desolate edge of society. Blaise Ferrage Seye was born in 1757 in Cessan, near Comminges, Southern France. He was a stonemason by trade and spent his spare time seducing the local women. He didn't worry whether they were married or single. So it was no surprise when one irate and powerful husband forced him to flee for his life into the mountains.

He made his home in a cave, then mused on the problem of surviving in the hostile terrain. At first he raided the local villages, stealing cattle and poultry, and when the mood took him he kidnapped young girls for sex – fending off pursuers with buckshot from his flintlock fowling gun.

On at least one occasion, when a girl attempted to escape his clutches, he shot her dead then had sex with her still warm body.

He lived as a bandit for three years, putting terror into the hearts of the local population.

As time went on, getting animals for food became harder and harder. Farmers banded together to protect their flocks and livestock, and nothing in the mountains was worth hunting.

So Seye, like Sawney Beane before him, hit on the logical solution: he'd hunt humans. It didn't take him long to start preferring human flesh to that of stringy old goat meat. And it turned out to be fun. He enjoyed the thrill of the chase, the pleasure of raping the women he caught, and the satisfaction of eating his prey.

But he came unstuck in 1782 when someone tipped off the authorities to the location of his cave. He was sentenced to a slow, torturous death. First he was put on the Catherine Wheel, on which all the bones in his body were broken. Then he was left on the gibbet to die. As he died he apparently gazed with enormous disdain at the huge crowd that had gathered to watch his execution. It was said he'd always been a misanthrope – he hated people. Maybe this explained his ugly stare. Or perhaps he was just put out that his chosen prey had finally turned the tables on him, and were killing him...

ALFRED PACKER

Another colourful cannibal was Alfred Packer. He was a poor Pennsylvanian who suffered from epilepsy, had missing front teeth and a crippled left hand. None of that stopped him serving in the Union Army and fighting in the American Civil War. After his honourable discharge, he journeyed to Colorado to make his fortune. Instead he wound up in a state penitentiary in Canon City on charges of murder and cannibalism.

The story began in autumn 1873. Packer, who was then in his mid-twenties, led a team of nineteen prospectors from Salt Lake City, Utah, to the San Juan mountains in the Colorado Rockies. Word had it that Packer had a good nose for gold and knew Colorado better than anyone. This was why the prospectors had hired him as their guide.

The team travelled for weeks through the barren terrain, loaded down with supplies and equipment. Tired and weary, the men came within sight of the snow-capped peaks. But by this time they were starving. Luckily they stumbled across an Indian camp. Although they expected to be killed, they had no choice but to enter the camp and ask for help. It turned out their luck was in. To their surprise the Indians were more than hospitable and fed and looked after them.

When the prospectors told them about the proposed

expedition, the Indian leader, Chief Ouray, strongly advised against the trip, which he said was far too risky during the winter months. He succeeded in persuading ten of the party not to go on what he described as a 'futile quest'. They cut their losses and returned to Salt Lake City.

Packer also wanted to abandon the mission. But those left offered to pay him well if he continued as their guide. Not one to turn down the offer of cash, he agreed.

The party remained at the Indian camp until they were fully recovered and ready to take on the arduous trip into San Juan country.

As the Indians couldn't dissuade them, they provided provisions and advised Packer and his band to follow the course of the Gunnison River. This, they said, was the safest route, given the treacherous winter conditions.

Packer had other ideas. He was always claiming he knew the region like the 'back of his hand' and told his group how rich seams of gold had recently been found close to the source of the Rio Grande. True to form he said he knew of a much shorter route to get there.

Four of the party decided to follow the advice of the Indians and follow the Gunnison River, while Packer led the remaining five men – Israel Swan, Frank Miller, George Noon, Shannon Bell and a man named Humphrey – on his route into the mountains.

Of the group who took the Gunnison River route, two died of starvation and exposure. The two surviving men – who had now completely abandoned any ideas of finding gold – finally made it to the Los Pinos Agency in February 1874. General Adams – who was in charge of the Agency which helped provide the local Indian reservation with education, medical help and agriculture – saw to it they were fed and brought back to health before sending them on their way back to civilisation.

In March of that year, on a cold, snowy morning, a wild, bedraggled man carrying a rifle turned up at the Agency begging for food and shelter. His face was bloated, but he was otherwise in good physical condition considering he'd been out in the wilds for some considerable time. It was Alfred Packer.

Adams was on business in Denver at the time. But his staff fed Packer and listened to his story. He claimed that his five companions had deserted him while he was ill, leaving him with a rifle so he could hunt wild game to survive.

He stayed at the Agency for ten days, then left saying he planned on visiting his brother's home in Pennsylvania. Before embarking on his journey, however, he decided he'd treat himself to a few drinks and hit the bars in nearby Saquache. He drank heavily and locals noted he appeared to have a good deal of money. While drunk, he told conflicting stories about the fate of his companions. Not surprisingly, people began to speculate that he had murdered them.

Word of this reached General Adams. He decided to have Packer tracked down and arrested. Then he set up a meeting between Packer and the men who had abandoned the mission. It soon became clear that his story was a pack of lies. And Packer didn't do himself any favours; he tended to come across as untrustworthy. In her 1884 book, *Tales of the Colorado Pioneers*, Alice Polk Hill described him this way: 'His features are not wholly bad, his nose is straight, his brow broad and suggestive of intellect. He wears his hair long, combed into a smooth deep scallop on his brow, and carried back behind his ears. He walks like one sneaking or creeping upon a victim. Anyone possessing even a moderate knowledge of human nature would say he belonged naturally to the criminal class.'

General Adams didn't hesitate. He had Packer tightly bound and taken back to the Agency, where he was kept in solitary confinement.

On 2 April 1874 two Indians ran into the Agency in a highly agitated state, clutching two strips of flesh, which they described as 'white man's meat'. They said they found it lying in the snow, just outside the Agency. As the weather had been extremely cold, it was well preserved. Packer must have been carrying it as rations to keep him going. Then dumped it when he got to the Agency.

When Packer was shown the flesh he let out a loud groan of despair, and sank to the floor. He was given restoratives. After coming round he begged for mercy and made the following statement:

When I and five others left Ouray's camp, we estimated that we had sufficient provisions for the long and arduous journey before us, but our food rapidly disappeared and we were soon on the verge of starvation. We dug roots from the ground upon which we subsisted for some days, but as they were not nutritious and as the extreme cold had driven all animals and birds to shelter, the situation became desperate.

Strange looks came into the eyes of each of the party and they all became suspicious of each other. One day I went out to gather wood for the fire and when I returned I found that Mr Swan, the oldest man in the party, had been struck on the head and killed, and the remainder of the party were in the act of cutting up the body preparatory to eating it. His money, amounting to $200,000, was divided among the remainder of the party.

The food only lasted a few days, and I suggested that Miller be the next victim because of the large amount of flesh he carried. His skull was split open with a hatchet as he was in the act of picking up a piece of wood. Humphrey and Noon were the next victims.

Bell and I entered into a solemn compact that as we were the only ones left we would stand by each other whatever befell, and rather than harm each other we would die of starvation.

One day Bell said, 'I can stand it no longer', and he rushed at me like a famished tiger, at the same time attempting to strike me with his gun. I parried the blow and killed him with a hatchet. I then cut his flesh into strips which I carried with me as I pursued my journey. When I espied the Agency from the top of the hill, I threw away the strips I had left, and I confess I did so reluctantly as I had grown fond of human flesh, especially that portion around the breast.

Packer then agreed to guide a party to where he had left the murdered men. He led them into the towering, inaccessible mountains, then claimed to be bewildered. It was decided that little would be gained by continuing and the search was called off, the plan being to head back to the Agency the following day.

That night Packer launched a murderous attack on one his guards and attempted to escape. But he was overpowered, bound, and taken back to the Agency. Then he was turned over to the sheriff.

In June 1874 the bodies of the men were found by an artist sketching along the shores of Lake Christoval. Four of them were lying in a row and the fifth, minus his head, was found a short distance away. The bodies of Bell, Swan, Humphrey and Noon had rifle bullet wounds in the back of their skulls. When Miller's head was found it was caved in, most likely from a blow from a rifle butt.

This totally contradicted Packer's statement.

A beaten path was found leading from the bodies to a nearby cabin, where blankets and other items belonging to the murdered men were found. It was clear that Packer had lived in the cabin for many days and had made frequent trips to the bodies for meat to eat. Each body had its breast sliced away to the ribs. Clearly Packer had been feasting on his favourite cut of human flesh.

The sheriff quickly got a warrant charging Packer with five murders. But during his absence Packer escaped and disappeared for nine years.

It was General Adams who first got wind of where Packer was. He received a letter on 29 January 1883, posted from Cheyenne in Wyoming. It was from a Salt Lake City prospector. He said he'd met Packer face to face in the area and that he was going under the name John Schwartze. The prospector also thought Packer had joined an outlaw gang.

Adams immediately sent word to the authorities in Cheyenne. Sheriff Sharpless of Laramie County set about tracking Packer down and finally arrested him on 12 March. He then took him to Lake City, Colorado, to stand trial.

Packer was charged with the murder of Israel Swan in Hinsdale County on 1 March 1874. His trial began on 3 April. The prosecution pointed out that each of the murdered men had been in possession of considerable sums of money and none of it had been found on their mutilated bodies. To them it was a clear case of murder for gain.

In his defence Packer said he had only killed Bell – and that was in self-defence. He described how his companions had fought amongst themselves and that Bell had fired at him. This, of course, completely contradicted what he had said in his original statement – which was why, on 13 April, the jury found him guilty and voted for the death penalty.

After appealing to the Supreme Court, however, Packer was granted a stay of execution. Once again it looked like he was going to get off lightly and – at least up to a point – escape justice. Not surprisingly the locals were enraged and Packer had to be transferred to Gunnison jail to keep him from the lynch mob.

In October 1885 he was granted a retrial. The prosecution decided their best option was to get him on five charges of manslaughter. They succeeded. Packer was found guilty on each charge and was sentenced to serve eight years for each offence, making a total of forty years in prison.

Sentencing, Judge Melville Gerry said, 'Packer, you man-eating son of a bitch, there were only seven Democrats in Hinsdale County and you, you bastard, ate five of them!'

Packer may have been one of America's most notorious criminals, but he was a model inmate. He never caused trouble and was mild-mannered and polite. He even became an expert gardener, lovingly caring for the flowers, shrubs and lawns in the state penitentiary.

Packer served seventeen years and protested his innocence throughout. He got out early because his case had been taken up by a crusading journalist who swayed public opinion around to the possibility that he might have been innocent after all. Eventually Packer's story was re-examined and he was pardoned on 1 January 1901.

It seemed that Packer might have been telling the truth when he said that a hunger-crazed Bell had killed and cannibalised the others, and that he had shot Bell in self-defence and only resorted to cannibalism as a last resort to survive the winter. But you could never tell with Packer, as events some eighty years later showed.

He died on a ranch near Denver on 24 April 1907, aged sixty-five. By rights that should have been that. But he was back in the news in 1989. A team of scientists had conducted a search of the scene of the murders, an area now known as Dead Man's Gulch. They used sophisticated radar to locate the remains of the victims (which had been left there by the original search team). They wanted to solve the 115-year-old mystery of whether Packer had murdered them or not.

The conclusion? 'Guilty as sin,' said James E. Starrs, a professor of law and forensic science at George Washington University, who led the expedition into the Rocky Mountains. He explained that the prospectors' bones provided scientific evidence that proves 'beyond the shadow of a doubt' that Packer killed the others and ate their flesh to stay alive. 'It is as plain as a pikestaff that Packer was the one who was on the attack, not Bell.'

The damage to the bones of the three victims, he went on, was 'caused with a hatchet-like instrument at a time when these persons were defending themselves from the attack of an aggressor.' In other words, the marks strongly suggested that the victims had raised their arms to ward off blows.

The team also found that the angle of the blade marks on the bones from which flesh had been taken – including the bones believed to be Bell's – indicated that the cuts were all made by the same person. Another very strong sign that Packer's version of events was false.

'Packer was having his fresh fillets morning, noon and night,' Starrs said, even though he could have survived by killing rabbits.

As far as Starrs was concerned Packer had been 'base, brutish and barbaric'.

Packer's guilt or otherwise was bound to lead to a certain amount of notoriety. Fan clubs devoted to his memory began to spring up. Folk singer Phil Ochs celebrated him during the early 1960s in a song called *The Legend of Alfred Packer*. Then in 1968 students at the University of Colorado at Boulder named their new cafeteria the Alfred Packer Grill.

Two movies have been made about his life: the first was *The Legend of Alfred Packer* which came out in 1980 and was directed by James W. Roberson; the second was a colourful musical about Packer's life called *Cannibal: The Musical*, which was directed and produced by Trey Parker and Matt Stone, creators of the animated *South Park* TV series. They also starred in the movie.

At one stage there was even an Alfred Packer online store – EveryThingAlferd.com – where you could buy souvenirs relating to the notorious cannibal. Note that the web address is not a typo. Packer often used to call himself – and sign his name – 'Alferd'. When young he'd had a tattoo done. But the tattooist – whether due to drink or illiteracy – misspelt his name. Fortunately for him, Packer saw it as a huge joke and happily adopted the new appellation.

GEORG GROSSMANN

Although he undoubtedly killed people, Packer could be described as the humorous face of cannibalism. You could see how an entertaining musical could be made about his life. But others in our round-up of historical cannibals would make an X-rated horror movie look like Noddy – particularly the terrifying flesh eaters that struck after World War I in Germany.

At that time the country's economy was in tatters, having lost the war. Inflation was running out of control. People had little money and food was short. Most cities were rife with criminal gangs and there was a huge black market in nearly everything.

Life was cheap. Muggings and assaults were commonplace. In the disorder, people sometimes also fell victim to murder. But when a number of cannibal killers came to light, it must have seemed like the country had been invaded by a band of human werewolves, intent on tearing into the delicate flesh of unwitting citizens.

One of these monsters was sadist and sexual degenerate Georg Grossmann, who prowled the slums of Berlin. He had a surly disposition which wasn't helped by the fact that he was large and ugly – and that bestiality numbered amongst his many perverted predilections.

He'd been convicted twenty-five times during his criminal career. Three of the convictions were for molesting children, one of whom he killed.

Born in Neuruppin in 1863, Georg had once been a butcher but hadn't managed to stick at it, favouring begging on the streets instead. Whenever he'd got money in his pocket he invariably spent it on low rent prostitutes, who had the unenviable task of satisfying his ugly needs.

Because of his criminal record he avoided military draft when World War I broke out. Around this time he dreamed up a way of turning his depraved appetites into profit.

He rented a squalid upstairs apartment in a downbeat part of Berlin, not far from the terminus of the Silesian railway. Gruff, morose and secretive, he was loathed by his neighbours. But because he paid his rent on time the landlord left him alone. Because his apartment had its own entrance his neighbours didn't see him much. But they certainly heard him – particularly during the early hours when he regularly stumbled home from late-night drinking bouts with giggling prostitutes clattering up the stairs.

He could afford all the booze and women he wanted now as he'd come up with a lucrative way to make money. Due to the food shortages people were struggling to find enough to eat. Georg, however, had the answer. He went back to being a butcher, peddling fresh meat on the streets. Unbeknown to his customers, however, the meat he was selling was of the human variety.

Georg didn't see why he or his fellow citizens should

starve. As far as he was concerned there was plenty of meat around; the streets were the equivalent of a pig pen, or a whole field of beef.

In August 1921, however, he came unstuck. His landlord heard the sounds of a violent struggle coming from Georg's apartment and called the police. When they arrived they found a freshly murdered woman in the kitchen, trussed up like a hog for the slaughter.

Evidence found in the apartment suggested he had killed at least three women in as many weeks. His diary, and statements he gave to the police, revealed he had sex with the women, slaughtered them, then sold their meat as fresh pork or beef. He disposed of what he called the 'useless' remnants in a nearby river.

True to form, Georg laughed when he was given the death sentence, probably because he planned to cheat justice by hanging himself in his cell.

KARL DENKE

Around the same time, a similarly depraved cannibal was on the loose in the appropriately named Munsterberg in Silesia, Germany – now Ziêbice, Poland. His name was Karl Denke and he is thought to have killed and eaten between thirty and forty people, most of whom were homeless. He also pickled his victims' flesh in jars and sold it on the Wroclaw market as 'boneless pork'.

Unlike Grossmann, Denke was well liked in his local community. In fact, people called him 'Vatter Denke' which meant 'Papa Denke'. He also served as the organ blower for his local church, helped carry the cross at funerals, and helped beggars and other people in need.

CANNIBALS

Karl came across as a kindly, avuncular figure who would not dream of hurting anybody.

Born on 12 August 1870 into a family of wealthy farmers, he was, however, something of a wild child, running away from home for a time at the age of twelve. He eventually settled down and, after graduating from elementary school, took up an apprenticeship as a gardener.

Karl was twenty-five when his father died. His older brother took over the farm. But Karl used some of his inheritance to buy a piece of land for himself. Unfortunately life as a farmer didn't work out and Karl was forced to sell his land. With the proceeds of the sale he bought a little house, with a shop attached, on Stawowa Street in Munsterberg.

In common with a lot of other people in Germany at the time, Karl's savings evaporated due to the rampant inflation that resulted after the country was defeated in World War I. He was forced to sell his house. Luckily he didn't have to move out. The new owner let him rent a little apartment on the ground floor, along with the small shop adjoining the house.

No one suspected that this pillar of the community had a terrifying dark side. Not until 1pm on 21 December 1924, that is, when vagrant Vincenz Olivier staggered into the police station, blood pouring from his open scalp, claiming that he had barely escaped with his life after being attacked by Karl Denke in his apartment. Police couldn't understand why Olivier was making such allegations. It couldn't be possible that Karl had mounted a vicious attack on the vagrant, could it?

After a doctor confirmed that Olivier was indeed seriously wounded the police decided to arrest Karl.

During the interrogation Karl claimed he had attacked the vagrant when he attempted to rob him after receiving a handout.

Karl was locked up in a holding cell, pending further investigations. That same night, at around 11:30pm, a police sergeant looked in on him and found him dead. Karl had hanged himself on a noose made from a handkerchief.

After Karl's body had been returned to his family, the police went to search his apartment and shop. They were shocked to the core. In the wardrobe hung dozens of bloodstained men's clothes, along with one skirt. On the windowsill were documents with the names of people released from prisons or hospitals. Karl had also listed the names and weights of people he'd killed and pickled. The list dated back to 1921 and gave the precise dates of the murders. It was like finding a Microsoft Excel file in a drug dealer's house listing all the dope that had been sold as well as to whom it had been sold.

What was truly terrifying, however, were the many jars of pickled meat, which a local chemist quickly confirmed were indeed of human origin. Alongside these was an array of bones awaiting thermal processing and equipment for making belts, leather straps and other products from human skin.

Karl was certainly enterprising. He'd been selling the meat at a local market – demand was great due to the rationing and shortages. His commercial activities had the full blessing and permission of city officials, none of whom were aware that he was peddling human meat. He even made use of human hair, processing it to make shoelaces which he sold door-to-door.

In the end police identified the names of twenty of Karl's victims, but believe he had pickled around forty people.

By hanging himself Karl had taken the mystery of why he'd resorted to such barbarism to his grave. Maybe it was simply down to financial necessity – who knows?

FRITZ HAARMAAN

Perhaps most notorious of all the cannibals at this time was the 'Butcher of Hanover', Fritz Haarmaan, who reputedly reached orgasm while he chewed his way through his victims' throats. Fritz was born in Hanover in Saxony on 25 October 1879. He was the sixth child of an ill-matched couple, a morose train stoker known as 'Sulky Olle' and his invalid wife, seven years his senior. She had become bed-ridden after Fritz was born. The couple didn't get on. They argued most about the children. Fritz became his mother's pet and came to despise his father. From an early age he took to playing with dolls and dressing as a girl.

At sixteen he was sent to a military school for NCOs at Neuf-Breisach, but was soon discharged after he showed signs of having epileptic fits.

His father gave him a job in the small cigar factory he started after leaving the railway. But the youth was lazy and took days off, which he spent indecently assaulting small children. When he was caught he was sent to an asylum for observation, but escaped after six months. He then took to petty crime and continued sexually assaulting minors.

He had a sexually normal period around 1900 when he became engaged to a girl he had made pregnant. But she bore a stillborn child and he broke off the engagement. After that he enlisted in the 10th Jaeger battalion, becoming an officer's batman. He served satisfactorily until 1903, then returned to Hanover, where his father tried to have him certified insane – unsuccessfully.

Fritz spent seven of the next twenty years in jail for burglary, fraud and indecency. He spent virtually the whole of World War I behind bars. On his release in 1918, he joined a meat smuggling ring and soon became prosperous – what with the food rationing and shortages after the war. He also became a police informer. Not for cash, but for immunity; his smuggling operation couldn't have survived otherwise. As a result, the police turned a blind eye both to his illegal business transactions and his sexual preferences.

He became so deeply immersed in the police system that people began referring to him as 'Detective Haarmaan'. It wasn't an ironic nickname. Many low-life types really believed he was in the police.

Fritz lived at 27 Cellarstrasse, deep in the warren of narrow streets in the slum quarter. It was close to the main Hanover railway station where he'd meet the incoming refugee trains to pick up youths, offering them lodgings for the night. One of the first of these was seventeen-year-old Friedel Rothe. The young man's parents had become worried their son was missing. Their enquiries revealed that Friedel had been friendly with 'Detective' Haarmaan. They contacted the police, who searched Haarmaan's room, but found nothing (Fritz later revealed that the boy's head lay wrapped in a newspaper behind the stove at the time). But they did catch Fritz having sex with another boy and he received nine months in jail for indecency.

Released in September 1919, Haarmaan moved to new

apartments in Neustrasse. Soon afterwards he took up with Hans Grans, a twenty-four-year-old gay man, pimp and petty thief. The two formed a dark alliance. They used to meet at the Café Kröpcke, a well-known hang-out for criminals and people with alternative sexual tastes.

The two always followed the same murderous pattern. They would entice a homeless youth from the railway station to Haarmaan's apartment, where he would be sodomised and killed. Haarmaan liked to dispatch them by biting through their throats in a werewolf frenzy of lust and death. The victim's body was then butchered and sold as meat on local market stalls. The clothes were also sold, while the uneatable portions of the carcass were thrown into the River Leine.

The victims ranged from ten to twenty years of age. Some were killed for no better reason than Hans taking a fancy to their trousers or shirts.

Haarmaan came close to discovery a number of times. He was once seen leaving his apartment carrying a bucket covered with a cloth. When the cloth blew off to reveal that the bucket was full with blood, Haarmaan just whistled cheerfully and walked on. His trade as a meat smuggler averted suspicion. On another occasion two friends of Grans visited his apartment in his absence and found a large amount of meat. They became suspicious and took a sample to the police. A police doctor reported that it was pork.

From 1918 to 1923 there was no physical evidence of Haarmaan's murders – although there must have been many – but from February 1923 there were twenty-seven disappearances in which Haarmaan was definitely involved.

One victim – a youth named Keimes – was found strangled and tied up in the canal. Curiously, not long after the seventeen-year-old was declared missing, Haarmaan called on his parents as a 'detective' and assured them he would locate their son in three days. He then went to the police and denounced Grans as the murderer. Grans was in prison at the time, so the allegation was dismissed as a gay lovers' quarrel.

In May 1924, a skull was found on the banks of the river and, a few weeks later, another one. On top of that, people continued to report missing sons.

People speculated about the fate of the missing boys and the grisly finds. Rumours circulated that human flesh was being sold at the station market. This led to a wave of hysteria spreading through Hanover, and even throughout Germany itself. Since the end of the war daily life had been an up-hill struggle anyway. Now – just when things apparently couldn't get any worse – there was some kind of beast on the loose.

Suspicion eventually fell on Haarmaan. But being a police informant he knew nearly all the local cops by sight. So two detectives from Berlin were called in to shadow him. Eventually they pulled him in on an indecency charge.

His apartment was searched and numerous items of clothing and possessions were found which turned out to have belonged to many of the missing boys. Even Haarmaan's landlady's son was found to be wearing a coat that had belonged to one unfortunate victim.

On top of all this, yet more bones were discovered by boys playing close to the river. A police pathologist said they represented the remains of at least twenty-seven bodies.

The net was finally closing in.

Seeing no way out, Haarmaan decided to confess. Part of his statement to police read:

I admit that I killed – possibly during the strange fits of madness that would overpower me at times – a number of youths whose names, with a few exceptions, escape me. I never wanted to kill them. They were mostly poor boys, and I honestly took them home with the intention of sheltering them and feeding them. But then we would get drunk and suddenly everything would go black. I would strangle them to death.

After that he would go to sleep for an hour or so – presumably the effort of killing and the sodomy that preceded it took it out of him. On waking, he would brew a pot of coffee before setting about dismembering the bodies.

'I disposed of the useless parts of the corpses,' he confessed, 'and prepared the rest for sale.' Chillingly, he ended his statement by saying, 'You see, gentlemen, I needed a million bodies.'

What for is anybody's guess. But my cannibal informant, Eric Soames, claimed that this statement was one of the many indications that Haarmaan was possessed by a demonic entity.

'It was the demon speaking through him,' Soames wrote when we discussed the case by email. 'The creature literally wanted to consume a million bodies. It would not have had any feelings for humans and would have seen them as a kind of spiritual food. The demon's host – Haarmaan – would physically eat the flesh, while the demon that possessed him would ingest the life force of the deceased. Such entities are essentially soul eaters.'

While I give some credence to the idea of prater human entities (my own experiments with magic suggest this could be possible) I generally consider that all these things reside firmly in our subconscious minds. Perhaps they are echoes or 'DNA memories' of our reptilian past, millions of years ago when life first pulled itself from the oceans. Wherever they spring from, the fact is they are dangerous. If elements of your deepest subconscious come to the fore your behaviour – *at the very least* – will be unpredictable.

The so-called 'great work' of magicians and occultists is to explore the recesses of the subconscious. Many, however, have been driven mad by what they found. This is not surprising. You can find great beauty in the deeper levels of yourself, but you can also find utter horror. You see your own potential to commit unimaginable atrocities. You encounter the beast within and see what it is capable of. You either deal with this; or you go mad.

Whether Haarmaan was literally possessed by a demon or whether the 'beast' aspects of his subconscious were coming to the fore is immaterial. In many respects it amounts to the same thing: the dark aspects of his soul had gained the upper hand and determined that he feed on his own kind.

Of course it is also possible that Haarmaan was simply joking when he said he needed a million bodies. During his trial, which began on 4 December 1924 and lasted fourteen days, he often laughed at odd or inappropriate moments, suggesting he was either insane or totally lacked remorse and found the whole thing funny.

Inexplicably, Haarmaan seemed to have the upper hand in court, with the judges and officials pandering to his every whim. When he complained that he was bored and demanded he be allowed to smoke in the dock, they let him light a cigar. When he complained that there were too many women in court lapping up all the gory details, one of the judges apologised because he didn't have the power to keep them out.

One hundred and thirty witnesses were called in total. Every so often Haarmaan took over the questioning of them. 'Now come on,' he would chide. 'You must tell us all that you know. We are here to hear the truth.' The judges apparently nodded in approval.

When Haarmaan denied one murder, the judges accepted it without question and instructed the jury to find him not guilty of it.

When he denied being mad or suffering from a nervous disorder, they murmured their agreement.

Clearly all this would have been highly distressing for the victims' loved ones. But it is possible the judges were pandering to Haarmaan for good reason. It might have been a ploy to ensure he didn't plead Not Guilty, which could have resulted in him not getting the death sentence. Either that or they were worried that Haarmaan's links with the police as an informer would come out if they opposed him in any way.

After being found guilty and sentenced to death, Haarmaan told the court, 'I want to be executed in the marketplace. On my tombstone must be put this inscription: "Here lies Mass-Murderer Haarmaan". On my birthday, Hans Grans must come and lay a wreath on it.'

Needless to say his requests were never acted on.

Haarmaan went to the guillotine to be decapitated on March 1925. His accomplice Hans Grans got off lightly. He received life imprisonment, but this was later reduced to twelve years.

EIGHT:
BEAST OF TORTURE

Sometimes... and there's no way to avoid it... you run into bad people. People so depraved they don't care whether you live or die. They just see you as a pleasure tool for their deranged lusts and hungers. You need to recognise them for who they are. See the evil inside. Then you need to get them first... before they get you.

If you'd run into Gary Heidnik back in the 1980s and you were a woman, you'd have wished to Hell that you'd been seriously tooled up. Serious firepower, knives... anything... so you could've have taken the motherfucker out.

He was the grim reaper come to town. But the women who came into his path went willingly to the torture house. If they didn't lose their lives, they lost their minds. And maybe you will just reading about him. But don't blame me. I'm just the storyteller.

Let's pick up the story on 24 March 1987, when black

streetwalker Josefina Rivera raced frantically... literally running for her life... through the streets of Philadelphia, Pennsylvania. Until at last – ragged, dishevelled and hysterical – she got to her destination: her boyfriend's apartment. She banged frantically on the door, whispering hoarsely, 'Please, please let him be in.'

When Vincent Nelson opened the door he couldn't believe his eyes. Josefina normally took such a pride in her appearance, but she had changed almost beyond recognition since he'd last seen her four months ago. They'd had a violent row and Josefina had stormed off into the bitterly cold November evening to ply her trade and pick up some 'johns'.

He hadn't thought much about her not coming back. He'd presumed the row was the 'break-up call' and she'd found some other guy.

She had. But it was a far cry from romance.

'What the fuck is this?' gasped Nelson, noting how excruciatingly thin and haggard Josefina was. It looked like she hadn't eaten properly for months. She also had terrible scars and sores around her ankles.

Recalling that fateful night, Nelson later revealed how Josefina had blurted out an incredible story of rape, torture and murder. 'She came in, she was rambling on, you know, talking real fast about this guy having three girls chained up in the basement of this house and she was held hostage for four months,' he said. 'She said he was beating them, raping them, and had them eating dead people... Dogs was in the yard eating people's bones. I just thought she was crazy...'

'Eating dead people? Dogs chomping on human bones? What was this?' Had she been watching too many horror movies and dropping acid?

In the end, Nelson agreed to go with her to a phone box to dial 911. Something had gone badly wrong for Josefina. That was for sure. So any help – even from the cops – had to be good. Not long after they got back to Nelson's apartment a squad car arrived with two officers – John Cannon and David Savidge – who listened to Josefina's story.

At first they were sceptical – presuming, like Nelson, that she was probably on drugs. But the scars around her ankles made them decide the story was worth checking out.

Josefina told the officers that she had been kidnapped on 26 November 1986 by a powerfully built white man with intensely blue eyes and a neatly trimmed beard, driving a Cadillac Coupé de Ville. She had been standing on a street corner with a group of other prostitutes. But the guy had called out to her – possibly because he had a penchant for pretty girls of mixed black and Hispanic heritage.

When she approached the big white Cadillac she could see the driver was not short of money. He was wearing a Rolex watch and lots of other expensive jewellery. She noted something odd too. Despite his display of wealth, it was clear the man hadn't showered or washed in days. He stank and his clothes were filthy.

Josefina had always prided herself on being choosy about her clients. But dirty or not, it made economic sense to go with this guy. What with his flashy car and gold rings she was sure to get a good fee out of him.

So she introduced herself as 'Nicole', then got into his car and they drove away. The first stop was McDonalds for a coffee, which was innocuous enough. But the second stop – the man's house on North Marshall Street, just three blocks away from where she was picked up – turned into a nightmare far worse than any video nasty could depict.

She told the two policemen how the man had viciously tortured and raped her, and how other women imprisoned in the building had been treated in a similar way. Worse still, Josefina said she had witnessed the murders of two of her fellow captives.

By this time, Cannon and Savidge were convinced. They phoned in their report and demanded an immediate search warrant and back-up to help them search the house once they had the kidnapper safely in custody.

Josefina had escaped the torture house by convincing her captor – whom she'd gradually persuaded to trust her – that if he took her home to see her family she could get him more women to serve his depraved needs. He'd often talked about abducting more women, so he readily agreed – on condition that if he dropped her off near her house she would meet him at midnight at a nearby gas station.

The police decided this would be a good place to lie in wait for him. So with Josefina in the back, Cannon and Savidge parked their cruiser across the street from the gas station. Not long after midnight, a white Cadillac drew up. Josefina said it was the man that had abducted her. Cannon and Savidge jumped out of the car with guns drawn, shouting, 'Get out of the vehicle with your hands up!' The man complied. Playing it cool, he casually asked, 'Hey, is this about overdue child support payments?'

'No,' growled Cannon. 'It's more serious than that.' The man gave his name as Gary Michael Heidnik, aged forty-three. He was taken into custody and removed to the Sex Crimes Unit at Headquarters.

Police kept Heidnik's house under observation while they obtained a warrant and put a search team together. The dilapidated two-storey brick house was situated in Franklinville, a disadvantaged district of Philadelphia made up mostly of low-income families and low-life, white trash. The windows were barred and a banner across the front stated United Church of the Ministers of God. The house was guarded by two savage dogs, a German shepherd and a Doberman.

It was approaching 5am when armed police finally kicked down the front door of 3520 Marshall Street. Josefina was with them. She pushed her way to the front and directed them down to the dingy basement, shouting, 'Hurry, there's women here needing a hospital!' Once there, the police found two naked black women. They were huddled together on a filthy mattress. To prevent escape they were shackled by the ankles to a large sewer pipe that ran up through the ceiling.

The women were terrified at first, but when they realised it was the police – and not some bizarre new torture routine from Heidnik – they kissed the officers' hands in gratitude, crying, 'Hosanna, we are free!'

When they had calmed down, Officer Savidge asked, 'Is there anybody else here?' With looks of sheer horror on their faces, the two women – one aged eighteen, the other twenty-four – pointed to a large piece of board on the floor.

'She's there, she's in the hole...' they said in unison.

It was Heidnik's 'punishment pit'.

Pushing the board aside police found a dark and dank hole. Inside was yet another naked black woman, curled up in a foetal position in the mud and slime. Like the other women she was shackled by the ankles but also had her hands cuffed behind her back.

After ambulances had taken the starved and terribly weak women to hospital, police began their search of the rest of the house. The first thing they found was a stack of pornographic magazines featuring black women. Clearly, the guy had a liking for black chicks. When they moved to the kitchen, the full horror of what had gone on became apparent. Inside a filthy and scorched cooking pot on the stove was a human skull, along with the gelatinous remains of human fat. In the fridge was a forearm, dripping in blood like a prime steak on the bone. There was also a heap of charred ribs and other selected cuts from an unfortunate victim. What's more, the food processor on the kitchen counter had clearly been used to grind meat – human meat – which had been neatly wrapped in plastic bags labelled 'dog food'. Nearby was a pile of arm and leg bones with varying amounts of flesh still clinging to them.

Unsurprisingly, more than one officer had to rush outside to vomit, such was their revulsion at the nightmarish scene they'd walked into.

Detective Lamont Anderson told reporters that other body parts had been found in the house, adding that they believed that at least two women had been killed in the basement. Not surprisingly the press had a field day, running headlines like 'Mad Man's Sex Orgy With Chained Women', 'Man Held In Torture Killings', and 'Women Held in Horror Dungeon'.

The media also made much of the fact that Heidnik was the head of his own invented church and was something of a whizz-kid with money. In the early 1970s Heidnik had gone to live in California, where he had founded the 'United Churches of the Ministries of God'. On his return to Philadelphia he duly registered the church, set himself up as 'bishop', and gathered together a flock of followers.

In 1975 Heidnik capitalised on his 'religious status' by opening an account with investment brokers Merrill Lynch in the name of his church. He was well aware that under US tax law churches don't pay income tax. Over the next twelve years his initial investment of $1,500 would grow to well over half a million. Heidnik flaunted his new-found wealth by buying a fleet of luxury cars. Apart from his favourite – the white Cadillac Coupe DeVille with gold-trim, custom wheels and a 'GMH' monogram on the front doors – he had a Rolls Royce and a Lincoln Continental.

Displaying his affluence didn't end there. Heidnik had glued coins on the kitchen walls of his house on Marshall Street, and had even papered the upstairs hallway with $1, $5 and $10 bills.

While the press continued to speculate and lap up the gory details, the police got down to the rigorous work of scouring every inch of the building for clues. Cardboard box after cardboard box was brought out of the house containing body parts, bloodstained clothing, assorted cooking utensils, and other vital evidence needing thorough analysis.

Meanwhile, the four surviving captives were questioned in hospital and the full sickening details of their ordeal began to come out. Three of the women had been imprisoned for three months. Their daily routine consisted of being tortured and raped by Heidnik, who fed them on a diet of dog food, bread and water. They were kept as sex slaves in the basement, and were only released from their shackles for yet more sex and torture upstairs. Police were shocked to discover that the starving captives had sometimes been fed on human flesh blended in a food-processor and mixed with dog food. One of Heidnik's dogs had even been seen chewing on a human leg bone...

One of the survivors, nineteen-year-old Lisa Thomas, described how she had seen a woman she knew only as 'Sandy' fall heavily to the floor after being handcuffed and chained from the ceiling. She smashed her head on the concrete floor rendering herself nearly unconscious. Unmoved, Heidnik simply pushed her into the 'punishment pit' and left her to die.

Sandy was later identified as Sandra Lindsay, aged twenty-four. Despite having mild learning disabilities, a speech impediment and slight limp, she had been motivated enough to take training classes in a bid to find a job that paid enough for her not to be a burden on her mother and siblings. Her fatal mistake had been to date Heidnik on and off. Sandy had even been pregnant by him, but opted to have an abortion – a decision Heidnik was furious about. Getting on the wrong side of Heidnik was clearly not wise – as Josefina made clear when she told police how he had boasted of having fed the boiled remains of Sandy to the rest of the starving women.

Police were also told of how twenty-three-year-old Debbie Dudley had been murdered. Because they'd done or said something to displease him, Heidnik had hurled three of the captives, including Debbie, into the punishment pit. He then ordered Josefina to fill it with water up to chin level. As if this wasn't punishment enough, he lowered an electric wire into the water – had Josefina switch on the power – and watched with mirth as the girls shrieked, screamed and jerked uncontrollably as currents surged through their already ravaged bodies. Heidnik told Josefina to cut off the power. But then decided one more jolt was needed to drive his point home. This time, however, the end of the electric cord touched the chain around Debbie Dudley's neck – and literally fried her.

Heidnik pulled her lifeless body from the pit, grinned broadly at the other girls, and said: 'Aren't you glad it wasn't one of you?'

HELL'S HAREM

As the details of the story emerged, it became clear that Heidnik was a monster of unbelievable proportions. If he had any humanity, it must have been hidden beyond reach in his troubled psyche. He picked up his first victim, Josefina Rivera, late at night on the eve of Thanksgiving, 1986. After taking her back to his house for sex, he grabbed her by the throat, handcuffed her and dragged her down to the basement, where he chained her up. She looked on in horror as he began digging a big hole in the concrete floor, fearing it was to be her grave. But Heidnik reassured her that the hole was only for punishment if she misbehaved. As he shovelled more dirt he told her he was only attracted to black women and that all he'd ever wanted was a big family. 'That's why I'm gathering a group of ten women,' he said. 'To keep them here in the basement and get them all pregnant. We'll all be one big happy family.'

He also told her that he'd served four years in prison after being found guilty of the rape of a mentally handicapped black woman, who was pregnant by him. The medical examination revealed the woman had been raped, sodomised, beaten and infected with gonorrhoea vaginally, anally and orally. Heidnik, however, considered it unfair because he believed the sex had been voluntary. He was also outraged by the fact that the daughter he had by the woman had been placed in care. 'Society owes me a wife and family,' he told Josefina. He then took a break from digging and made her perform oral sex on him before raping her.

Later that day Josefina saw a chance for escape. She managed to force open a boarded-up window and screamed for help. Nobody took any notice. Except Heidnik, that is, who came down and beat her with a board, then threw her into the punishment pit – securing the lid with heavy bags of dirt. He brought a radio down and cranked it up to full blast to muffle her screams.

Three days later, on 29 November, Heidnik brought his second prisoner down to the basement. This was Sandy Lindsay. She'd been walking to a local drugstore when Heidnik pulled up asking if she wanted a lift. As she'd known him for years and he was a 'friendly face', she said, 'Yeah, sure.' Once he'd got her back to the house on Marshall Street he dragged her down to the basement and stripped her of everything but her blouse, then shackled her to the sewage pipe.

Sandy's mother, however, got concerned when her daughter failed to return home. She called the cops who searched the neighbourhood. When news of Sandy's disappearance started being featured in local newspapers and on TV, Heidnik forced Sandy to write to her mother, saying she was all right and had gone away for a while and would call her soon. Heidnik posted the letter from New York to put the police off the scent.

Heidnik wasn't as clever as he thought he was. Sandy's mother told police her daughter had often mentioned a guy named Gary Heidnik who lived somewhere on Marshall Street. The police followed up the lead and made regular visits to Heidnik's house. Because no one ever answered the door, they gave up. There weren't any firm grounds to get a search warrant, so they abandoned that line of enquiry. The likelihood was Sandy would turn up somewhere else.

So life for the two incarcerated women continued to follow a similar pattern of daily beatings and forced sex, juxtaposed with a diet of oatmeal and bread. The cold, grimy basement – lit only by a naked bulb – must have seemed like hell itself to them.

On 22 December Heidnik brought back another captive – nineteen-year-old high school dropout Lisa Thomas. Although she was on social security she lived to the full and dressed in flashy clothes, which may have been what attracted Heidnik to her as he cruised up to her in his Cadillac. 'Hey, baby,' he said, 'are you hooking?'

Lisa saw red and stormed off. But Heidnik coasted the vehicle alongside her, saying, 'I'm sorry I was rude, how about I give you a ride to make up for it?'

Noting Heidnik's car and expensive jewellery, she finally agreed and got in beside him. This time round Heidnik wasn't in a rush. He wined and dined her first and even offered to take her to Atlantic City the following weekend. Quick to capitalise, Lisa said she didn't have any clothes to wear for the trip. So Heidnik took her shopping at the local Sears Roebuck store. She must have thought she'd fallen on her feet – which was probably why she made the biggest mistake of her life and agreed to go back to Heidnik's house.

Once there Heidnik kept up the romantic act and cracked open a bottle of wine. But the wine was spiked and Lisa soon passed out. When she woke up Heidnik was taking her clothes off. But this didn't worry her. She just assumed the wine had made her doze off. And besides she'd pretty much decided to have sex with the guy after spotting his flashy rings and Rolex watch. But when he dragged her down to the basement and chained her up with Josefina and Sandra, she soon wised up to how bad the situation was.

To be fair to Heidnik he did make one concession for the comfort of his growing group of 'wives'. While he wasn't concerned about the sheer filth and grime in the basement (no surprise, he wasn't even worried about his own personal hygiene), he did buy the girls a portable camper toilet for them to use.

On New Year's Day 1987 it was time to add yet another addition to his harem. At twenty-three, Deborah Dudley was a pretty girl. But with her strong will and fiery temper she wasn't going to give up without a fight. She bit and scratched at Heidnik in a desperate bid to avoid getting hauled down to the grim basement. Inevitably, after overpowering her, Heidnik beat her senseless as punishment.

It didn't take long for Heidnik to go after another victim. This time – on 18 January – he picked up eighteen-year-old streetwalker Jacquelyn Askins, a tiny girl with mental disabilities. Her ankles were too thin to be shackled, so Heidnik used handcuffs. As usual he gave her a severe beating, then told her, 'You'll do as you're told, or you'll get more of the same.'

By this time Heidnik had come to trust Josefina. He let her out of the basement to have meals with him, and gave her the responsibility of keeping an eye on the other captives – the idea being to report any talk of escape attempts. One attempt she reported led to a horrific punishment that would make even Saddam Hussein's notorious torture chambers look mild in comparison. Because there were now five of them, the women reasoned that together they should be able to overpower their jailer and make their getaway. Heidnik was livid when Josefina told him about it. First he beat the schemers senseless, then came up with a solution to prevent them even contemplating escape. If they couldn't hear him coming or going, he reasoned, they could never be certain when it was safe to attempt escape. So Heidnik opened up his toolbox, pulled out a screwdriver and rammed it deep into each of the girls' ears to rupture their eardrums and deafen them for life. Only Josefina, who had informed on them, avoided the punishment.

Such was Heidnik's trust in Josefina that he was now taking her out to fast food joints for a meal or for rides in his Cadillac or Rolls Royce. On 23 March he took her out in his car with him, and together they picked up yet another prisoner, Agnes Adams, aged twenty-four, another prostitute. She was needed because, by then, two of the other captives were dead – Sandy from cracking her skull on the basement floor and Debbie from electrocution.

Heidnik had disposed of Sandy by first cutting her body into pieces with a power saw and then grinding up what he could in a food processor. Lastly he boiled her head in a pan on the stove. Not surprisingly, neighbours complained about the obnoxious stench of overcooked meat. But when a cop dropped in to investigate, Heidnik told him he'd burnt his dinner. The officer didn't trouble to look in the saucepan on the stove.

As it was, the ground-up meat from Sandy was mixed with dog food and fed to both the dogs and the captives alike. As if torture and rape weren't enough, those left alive were forced to become cannibals.

That wasn't the extent of the horror, however. Not long after Heidnik finished chopping up Sandy's body, one of his dogs wandered into the basement carrying a large, meat-covered bone. Settling down in a corner he set about gnawing on it. Looking on in wide-eyed horror, the surviving captives vomited uncontrollably.

Josefina had accompanied Heidnik when he buried Debbie Dudley in a New Jersey park on 22 March. On the way back to Marshall Street he stopped off at a newsstand to buy a newspaper. 'I want to check my stocks,' he told Josefina casually.

BEAST IN CHAINS

Although she'd snitched on her fellow prisoners, which led to terrible punishments, Josefina was only doing what she could to find a way to escape. Not just for her sake, but for the others too. Clearly, a terrible price was paid to gain Heidnik's trust in terms of the other women being beaten and the screwdriver being twisted into their ears. But what other choice did Josefina have? They would have all been dead if she hadn't inveigled her way into Heidnik's good books.

So on 24 March Josefina finally gained her freedom, and

that of her fellow captives, by convincing Heidnik to take her home to see her family and agreeing to meet him at midnight at a nearby gas depot – where the cops picked him up.

When arrested Heidnik had almost two thousand dollars in cash on him, along with a whole stack of credit cards. There were papers on four cars, and a statement from the stockbrokers Merill Lynch showing his account standing at $577,382.52. At least his small fortune would be enough to buy the services of a good lawyer. Chuck Peruto was one of Philadelphia's top legal eagles and charged accordingly. His fees for a capital offence were $10,000, plus expenses.

But even lawyers can be choosy. Although Peruto believed everyone – even the lowest of the low – deserved the best legal defence money could buy, he drew the line at Heidnik. And besides he could well do without the negative publicity surrounding the case. So he told Heidnik his fee was $100,000, plus expenses. He was probably hoping it would put Heidnik off. It didn't. Heidnik wasn't a fool. He knew he needed all the legal help he could get if he was to avoid the electric chair.

Money, however, proved no protection from his fellow prisoners who were outraged by his crimes. On 25 March, within hours of his arrest, Heidnik got a taste of his own medicine. A group of fellow prisoners cornered him and gave him a severe beating, breaking his nose in the process. He was immediately placed in isolation for his own protection. Just over a week later – on 2 April – Heidnik decided he couldn't take any more and tried to hang himself in the shower, but prison guards got there just in time and revived him.

Meanwhile, detectives were looking into Heidnik's background. Born in November 1943 in Cleveland, Heidnik was the product of a broken home. His parents, both severe alcoholics, separated when he was two years old and his mother committed suicide in 1970 when she learned she had cancer. As a child he had been ridiculed for the shape of his head: local kids called him 'football head'. But the shape had been caused by injuries he got after falling from a tree.

Although he was bright, his loveless childhood left him too emotionally damaged to do well at school and he retreated into a fantasy world. He was also a bed-wetter, which infuriated his hard-drinking father who beat his son mercilessly. After his son's arrest, his father told the press: 'I hope to hell they hang him, and you can quote me on that. I'll even pull the rope.'

According to Gary Heidnik's younger brother, Terry, however, their father was not entirely without blame – particularly in respect to the attitudes he espoused. He would tell his two sons that 'life has no value if it's a black life'. His prejudices were a reaction to the affairs his alcoholic wife had with black men after the couple divorced in 1946. Gary Heidnik adopted the racist views of his father. Not only were all his victims black, but the act of shackling them was a direct mirror of the way slaves had been treated.

After dropping out of high school in 1961, at the age of eighteen, the young Heidnik joined the army. His army aptitude test revealed he had an above-average IQ of 130, enabling him to train as a medic. After finishing medical training he was stationed at a field hospital in West Germany where he seemed to be getting his life together. But then on 25 August 1962 he complained to an army doctor that he was suffering from headaches and dizzy spells. This led to him being shipped back to the USA for tests. Heidnik was diagnosed as having a borderline psychotic condition that 'often precedes breakdown to full schizophrenia'. On 23 January 1963 he was given an honourable discharge. Because his condition was considered service-related, he was also awarded a one hundred per cent mental disability pension for life.

Following his discharge Heidnik settled in Philadelphia. By the beginning of 1964 – making the most of his army medical qualifications – he enrolled for training as a practical nurse. After graduating a year later he took an internship at Philadelphia General Hospital, as well as studying as a part-time student at the University of Pennsylvania. He eventually took a job at the Elwyn Institute, a training facility for mentally and physically handicapped people. By all accounts he got along well with staff and students. He worked hard and saved his money, which enabled him to buy a big house in a ghetto neighbourhood where he rented out two apartments and lived in the third.

Despite this apparent stability, Heidnik still had to have time off work for treatment in psychiatric hospitals. When he got word of his mother's suicide in 1970, he took it badly and had a severe breakdown, which led to him being institutionalised. While in care he attempted suicide and fell into a near catatonic state. After responding to treatment he was well enough to be released. Feeling he needed a complete change he went to California and set up his 'United Churches of the Ministries of God'. According to people who knew him, the services he held for his flock on his return to

Philadelphia were genuine. He may well have believed what he was preaching. But his money-making ventures included less than holy activities like bingo and lone-sharking. It was the money from these enterprises that made him a small fortune after he invested it on the stock market.

By 1976 Heidnik was a wealthy man – such was his acumen with money. But that same year he had his first run-in with the law. He had rented out an apartment to a man, but when the guy climbed in through the window one night Heidnik opened fire on him with a revolver. Maybe he thought it was somebody breaking in. Either way, he was arrested for brandishing a firearm on a public street. Luckily for him the charge of assault with a deadly weapon was dropped.

Heidnik also began to display other worrying traits. On 7 May 1978 he broke a black woman out of the mental institution she lived in and hid her at his home. He knew her because she was the sister of the woman he'd had a child with (which had duly been put into care). As far as Heidnik was concerned he was doing her a favour. But when police located the woman it was clear she'd been seriously abused, both physically and sexually. As a result of his actions, Heidnik was convicted of unlawful imprisonment and deviant sex. In November 1978 he was sentenced to a maximum of seven years in the state penitentiary, but got out after four.

After being released on parole on 12 April 1983, aged forty, he bought the house on Marshall Street. He made up for the lack of sex in prison with a vengeance. Nearly every night he would have three-in-a-bed sex, always with black women and always deviant and abusive.

Deciding he wanted a Filipino wife, Heidnik went through a matchmaking service specialising in introducing Oriental women to Western men. After a two-year correspondence – in which he told her he was a minister – Heidnik invited twenty-two-year-old Betty Disto to come to Philadelphia. Four days after her arrival – on 3 October 1985 – the two drove out to Maryland where they were married. Two weeks later Betty discovered it was not a match made in heaven. Returning from a shopping trip she found her new husband in bed with three black women.

Heidnik tried to assure her that this was a normal custom for American males. She wasn't convinced and demanded he send her home. Heidnik refused, saying, 'If you don't wanna join in, you can just watch while we get it on.' When she complained, he beat her up. On another occasion he raped her anally while the other girls watched.

Finally, after more than a year of abuse and torment, Betty left Heidnik – but not before filing charges of spousal rape, indecent assault and involuntary deviant sexual intercourse. Two weeks later Heidnik was arrested. But he got lucky, avoiding a return to prison because Betty failed to turn up for his arraignment. All he got hit for was a weekly maintenance payment of $135. But he could afford it.

In November that same year, Heidnik climbed into his silver-white Cadillac and hit the streets to find the first candidate for his 'happy family'. At around the same moment, Josefina Rivera stormed out of her boyfriend's place, following a fierce argument, and walked into a fate worse than even Wes Craven could have dreamed up in his gruesome horror flicks.

Gary Heidnik's trial began on 20 June 1988 in

Philadelphia City Hall, room 653, before woman judge, Lynn Abraham. It was clear from the start that the defence counsel, Charles Peruto, would pin everything on an insanity plea in a bid to keep Heidnik out of the electric chair.

However, Assistant District Attorney Charles Gallagher, the chief prosecutor, was determined to get Heidnik the death penalty. He insisted that Heidnik had been too methodical in the execution of his crimes not to have been completely aware of what he was doing. He said Heidnik had murdered, raped, kidnapped and sexually assaulted six young women between the ages of eighteen and twenty-five.

'Gary Heidnik took these women home,' he told the jury. 'Then he plied them with food and in some cases sex. He assaulted them. He chocked them. He handcuffed them and took them to his basement, where he put shackles on their ankles? He starved them. He tortured them. He repeatedly had sex with them.'

Gallagher paused for a moment – milking the sudden silence for dramatic effect – then added that Heidnik had killed two of them, one of whose bodies he dismembered, cooked, and fed to the others.

The jury looked on in disbelief.

Gallagher let the sheer horror of it sink in, then continued. 'The evidence will show that from the eve of Thanksgiving 1986 up through 25 March 1987, the defendant committed repeated and sadistic malicious acts. He did them in a methodical and systematic way. He knew exactly what he was doing and he knew it was wrong. He took advantage of underprivileged people.'

In other words Heidnik was a callous, calculating monster, not a madman.

When Chuck Peruto rose for the defence he had a arduous task ahead. The first thing he did was make it clear that his client was not innocent. 'He is very, very guilty,' he said. He then told the jury that it was his job to show them inside Heidnik's head – to make them recognise that he simply wasn't sane.

'This is not a whodunnit,' he said. 'If all we had to decide here was who did it and what was done, it would be easy. You're not here to determine if Gary Heidnik is going to walk out of here a free man. He's never going to see the light of day. He will be put behind bars or in some mental institution. Any person who puts dog food and human remains in a food processor and calls it a gourmet meal and feeds it to others is out to lunch.'

Peruto told the jury that they needed to understand two things: 'One, Gary Heidnik didn't want anybody to die, and two, because of his mental illness he couldn't tell right from wrong.'

He then called expert witnesses to testify that Heidnik was mentally unbalanced at the time of the kidnappings and torture. One spoke at length about schizophrenia as a general condition. While another – a noted Philadelphia psychologist – didn't even make the stand due to Judge Abraham ruling that the majority of his testimony was inadmissible.

It didn't look good for Heidnik. Unsurprisingly, the most damning evidence came from the surviving women's account of their ordeal at the hands of Heidnik. But the testimonies from experts – on behalf of the prosecution – were equally horrific and chilling. Dr Paul Hayer, of the county medical examiner's office, described the gruesome finds in Heidnik's kitchen. He said that Sandy Lindsay's body parts appeared to have been cut from her corpse with a power saw, just as the surviving women had claimed.

Gallagher's final witness was not involved with forensics or psychology. Robert Kirkpatrick had been Heidnik's broker at Merrill Lynch. He testified that Heidnik was 'an astute investor who knew exactly what he was doing'.

The words 'knew exactly what he was doing' must have hung in the minds of the jury. On 20 June – after ten days of gruelling testimony and arguments – the jury retired to agree a decision. Sixteen hours later they found Gary Heidnik guilty in the first degree on all eight counts, including murder, rape, kidnapping, aggravated assault, deviant sexual intercourse, false imprisonment and indecent exposure.

The jury then deliberated the penalty. Under Pennsylvanian law, if a jury returns a guilty verdict for first degree murder they must also decide the penalty. The choices are life imprisonment or the death penalty. The jury came back the following day having decided on the latter.

But like many prisoners on death row, Heidnik had a long wait before meeting his maker. One appeal after another wound its way through the court system, giving Heidnik plenty of time to contemplate his sins in Graterford Prison at Rockview, Pennsylvania. Finally, on 6 July 1999 at 10:29am he was executed.

No one came forward to claim his body. Even his father rejected him when, over a decade earlier, reporters asked for his reaction at his son being given the death penalty. 'I'm not interested,' he said. 'I don't care. It doesn't bother me a bit.'

But what led Heidnik to commit such heinous acts on his

fellow human beings? Could he really have been sane, as the prosecution alleged? One psychiatrist, called by the defence team during Heidnik's trial, argued a convincing case for schizophrenia and split personality. He said that in Heidnik's head there existed an adult brain and a brain that was only seventeen months old. It was this infantile part of the brain which had kidnapped and raped the women.

While this might sound like a convenient get-off clause, studies in hypnosis have shown that people can be regressed back to childhood, causing them to display exactly the behaviour they would have when they were an infant. So it is not impossible that Heidnik could have reverted to an early childhood mindset and, during those phases, was unable to think and reason in an adult way.

His unconscious mind would have enabled him to function physically as an adult – in the same way that your unconscious mind drives your car when you're busy thinking deeply about something else and have no conscious knowledge of having driven the last five miles. But otherwise he may have been completely oblivious to his adult self, and literally may not have known right from wrong – as a seventeen-month-old infant wouldn't.

The head injury Heidnik received during childhood – the one that resulted in him being called 'football head' by other kids – may also have had a bearing on his possible schizophrenic condition. Studies have shown that a high percentage of serial killers have a history of head injuries.

Or are such theories just too complex – could Heidnik simply have been a monster, a random quirk of evolution?

Certainly, as far as Josefina Rivera was concerned, the motivation behind his crimes was simple. 'He got [his ideas] from watching TV,' she said during Heidnik's trial. 'He got the idea of feeding us parts of Sandy's body from *Eating Raoul*, and his ideas on punishment from *Mutiny on the Bounty*. He also saw *The World of Susie Wong* and he liked the way Oriental women were. That's why he picked a Filipino wife.'

In the end justice had to be seen to be done. Which was why, sane or not, Heidnik had to receive the death penalty.

FEMALE COUNTERPARTS

Heidnik epitomised the idea of male domination and sadism against women. But he does have female counterparts who have turned their wrath on men – and in some cases eaten them. It was a shame he didn't meet one. But like all sadists he chose his victims carefully and made sure they were vulnerable and not good at fighting back.

The vast majority of cannibals on record have been men. But members of the fairer sex have feasted on forbidden flesh. In 1981, Dutch woman, Anna Zimmermaan, a separated mother of two, got bored of her lover. Instead of writing him a 'Dear John' note, she drugged him and then drowned him in her bathtub.

After carving up his body, she consumed it in the form of roasts and steaks. She confessed to this act of cannibalism and also admitted murdering and eating her pets, explaining that it kept her butcher bills down. Authorities concluded she was insane, which, given the circumstances, seems like a fair assessment.

Another case hit the headlines in 1993 when Rocky Mountain police found fifty-one-year-old Peter Green's torso in a cupboard, his legs in the rubbish bin and his flesh in a saucepan. The pan belonged to Carolyn Gloria Blanton, who joined the female cannibal club after shooting Green, then cooking up and eating chunks of his body. She later told deputies that Green was in heaven and happy. After extensive evaluation, psychiatrists determined that Blanton was legally insane when she killed Green.

In 2006, in Bashkortostan, Russia, a woman was given an eleven-year sentence for killing her boyfriend with an axe and then cooking up parts of his body in a variety of dishes, which she fed to guests at a dinner party she hosted.

The forty-four-year-old woman (who has never been named) suspected her boyfriend, who was younger than her, of being unfaithful. During a heated row she grabbed an axe and hacked him to death. She then dismembered his body, threw away the head, and used what was left to cook up a New Year's celebration dinner. She minced up some of the body parts to make meatballs, and made jellied meat with her boyfriend's hands and feet.

When the guests arrived, the woman treated them to everything she had cooked: meatballs, dumplings, soup and liver sausage. None of them knew they were eating human flesh. One guest commented that the meat was unusually sweet; the woman told him this was because it was very fresh.

As the party drew to a close, one of the guests looked into the fridge and found a severed hand. He immediately called the police. During the first round of questioning the woman broke down and confessed to her gruesome deeds.

A similar incident occurred in Nepal in 2004. Indira Ghimere, a mother of four, allegedly cooked and ate parts of her husband's body after killing him and locking herself up in her room for five days. When police broke through the padlocked door, they found the skull of her forty-eight-year-old husband – an employee of Nepal's state-run food corporation – simmering in a pressure cooker. The rest of his remains were in a gas tank and a jug was filled with his blood.

The police were called after Indira's daughter and three sons complained they had not seen their parents and neighbours reported a foul smell.

KATHY THE CANNIBAL

Perhaps the most famous female cannibal, who strictly speaking didn't actually consume her lover's flesh, was Kathy Knight – better known as 'Kathy the Cannibal'. On the night she turned into a black widow, Kathy Knight slipped on the short sexy black nightie she'd left at the foot of the bed. The forty-five-year-old had bought it recently with the intention of seducing her lover John Price, known as 'Pricey', who was fast asleep. Kathy climbed into bed beside him, gently waking him up.

'Where are the kids?' asked Pricey, forty-four, who had gone to bed around 10pm, an hour earlier. Kathy told him that Natasha, her nineteen-year-old daughter, was looking after them at her house. 'So we've got some privacy.' Aroused at the thought, Pricey rubbed his hand over Kathy's stomach, now rounded by middle-age and four pregnancies.

Both had been married before and had got together in 1994. Each had their own modest property in the small, sleepy town of Aberdeen, which lies 266 kilometres north-north-west of Sydney, Australia.

Kathy regularly stayed at Pricey's bungalow – so much so that she usually referred to it as 'their' place, rather than as his. The relationship was very turbulent, with lots of fights and arguments. One issue that really lit the fuse was Kathy's demands on Pricey to either marry her or make the bungalow legally half hers. She felt entitled now they'd been together six years. Pricey always refused point blank. As far as he was concerned, any rights to the place should go to his children, not Kathy.

Because of her continual demands and the resulting conflict, Pricey was beginning to think he ought to end his relationship with Kathy once and for all. What really made up his mind was an incident that occurred a week earlier. Kathy had gone into a rage and had threatened him with a knife, forcing him to flee to a neighbour's house.

Everyone in Aberdeen knew Kathy was hot-tempered and that it was not a good idea to cross her. But most said, 'Well, that's just Kathy for you.' Nobody's perfect.

This was pretty much how Pricey saw it too. But now, the good-natured man who everyone described as a 'top bloke', was beginning to fear for his life. There was something about Kathy's outbursts that seemed not quite normal – not even for a rough and ready town like Aberdeen, dominated by mining and meat production industries.

After the knife incident, Pricey said to his workmates at Bowditch Construction: 'What if I wake up with a knife in my back?'

Yet on the night of 29 February 2000, when Kathy slipped on her sexy nightie, it must have seemed to Pricey that they had put their problems behind them. Little did he know that Kathy's seduction of him had the deadly intent of a praying mantis.

'He had sex with me and I had sex with him,'

Kathy recalled later. 'He went for a pee. I remember him coming back.'

After Pricey climbed back into bed, satiated after the sex, Kathy reached for a knife she'd concealed earlier. With expert precision, the one-time abattoir worker plunged the blade deep into Pricey's chest. She stabbed once, twice, three times... each strike spattering blood across the bed and walls.

Shaking with shock and horror, Pricey managed to heave himself out of bed and stagger out to the hallway. Kathy followed him, stabbing relentlessly at his back, shoulders and buttocks. Pricey neared the front door – escape was in his sights. But Kathy plunged the blade into his neck, spurting arterial blood over the walls and carpet.

Pricey was in a very bad way. Both his lungs had been punctured and the lower half of one kidney had been sliced off. It was a miracle he was still alive. With one last almighty effort, he attempted to throw himself out of the front door. But Kathy dragged him back inside and unleashed a final, frenzied attack.

Eventually, Pricey collapsed dead on the hallway floor. He'd been stabbed thirty-seven times. But Kathy wasn't done with him yet.

Somewhere between midnight and 3.30am, Kathy used her butchery skills to carefully strip the skin off Pricey's body. She then cut off his head and sliced off sections of his buttocks to prepare a grisly, cannibalistic meal for his children. She even set individual places for them at the dining table...

Meanwhile Pricey's workmates and his boss were starting to worry. Pricey hadn't turned up for work. And this was unlike him. You could set your watch by him when it came to being on time. What was really praying on their minds was Pricey telling them how Kathy had recently gone at him with a knife.

By 7.45am they decided to call the police who, on finding blood on Pricey's front door, broke in. They were confronted with a terrifying sight. Bubbling away on the stove was Pricey's head and sections of his buttocks were being cooked up with vegetables. Worse still, his skin – with face, hair, genitals, fingers and feet still intact – was hanging on a stainless steel hook in the lounge. His raw, blood-drained torso was close by.

It was a sight that would haunt officers for years to come.

Kathy was found slumped on the bed in a drug-addled stupor, pill bottles all over the floor. She had taken a non-lethal overdose in a fake suicide attempt to gain sympathy.

The strategy failed miserably.

When she went on trial in 2001, Supreme Court judge Barry O'Keefe sentenced her to life imprisonment, never to be released. In his summing up he said Kathy's evil actions stemmed from Pricey's refusal to share his assets with her, particularly the bungalow. 'I am satisfied beyond doubt that, not only did she plan the murder, but she also enjoyed the horrific acts which followed in its wake as part of a ritual of death and defilement.'

Chillingly, Kathy was found to be perfectly sane. Robert Delaforce, one of the psychiatrists brought in to assess Kathy's mental state, said: 'What she did on the night was part of her personality, her nature, herself.'

Kathy Knight and Gary Heidnik would have made a good pair. If he hadn't been executed they could have been put in a cell together. The result would have been interesting...

NINE:

GENERATION CANNIBAL

JEFFREY DAHMER

The problem with cannibal killers – and, indeed, psychopathic killers in general – is they usually appear perfectly normal. Harmless even. They don't look like monsters, even though that's exactly what they are inside. Jeffrey Dahmer was like that. He looked average – a regular guy. If you'd seen him in 1991, before his arrest, you'd never have guessed that he was about to go down in history as America's worst cannibal serial killer.

Dahmer came unstuck on 22 July 1991. It was a hot and sticky summer's night. Two cops were driving down North 25th Street, situated in one of the rougher areas of Milwaukee. Suddenly a half-naked black guy ran into their path. He was wearing handcuffs. 'Christ,' breathed the cop who was driving, as he slammed on the brakes.

The two cops then jumped out of the car to find out what was going on.

'A fucking freak put these cuffs on me,' the black guy blurted out. 'Get them off me – *please...*'

Presuming it was a lovers' tiff, they went over to the apartment which the man, whose name was Tracey Edwards, claimed to have escaped from – 213 Oxford Buildings – to check it out.

They banged on the door. It was opened by a clean-cut, polite young man called Jeffrey Dahmer. Considering the neighbourhood, his apartment was surprisingly neat and tidy.

Dahmer assured the officers there was nothing to worry about and said he'd find the key to unlock the handcuffs.

As they thought, just a lovers' tiff... But then one of the cops spotted a large knife under the bed. And in the top drawer of a nearby cupboard he noticed piles of Polaroid photos of naked men. A closer look revealed there were also shots of body parts, decomposing torsos and severed heads. Sickeningly, some of the photos were of Dahmer having sex with dead bodies.

The two immediately moved to arrest Dahmer. He put up a brief struggle. But within seconds they pinned him face down on the ground and handcuffed him.

While one of the cops called for back-up, the other took a look around the rest of the apartment. After a brief survey of the kitchen he opened the fridge, recalling that the black guy had said something about seeing something 'nasty' inside. He leapt back in horror. Staring up at him was the severed head of a black man, neatly packaged in a cardboard box.

Dahmer's horrific killing spree was about to be unravelled. In the days that followed, the Milwaukee police department and forensic teams scoured every inch of his apartment. The grisly finds they took away for analysis beggared belief. They included:

* A freezer containing three more heads
* Chemicals for preserving human body parts
* A complete skeleton
* A fifty-seven-gallon blue plastic drum containing three human torsos in various stages of decomposition
* Zip-locked bags stuffed with human flesh
* Dried genitals and hands
* Seven bleached human skulls.

Dahmer admitted to committing seventeen murders over the previous thirteen years. He'd killed his first victim in June 1978, when he was eighteen. While out driving he spotted a casual acquaintance, Steve Hicks, also eighteen, who was hitchhiking to his girlfriend's house. Dahmer offered to buy him a beer at a local bar. In no particular hurry, Hicks said, 'Yeah, why not.'

After a few beers they drove over to where Dahmer was living for more booze and to smoke marijuana. When Hicks decided it was time to go, things got out of hand. 'The guy wanted to leave,' Dahmer told the cops thirteen years later, 'and I didn't want him to.'

Dahmer's solution to keep him there was to batter him to death with a barbell.

He had a pathological fear of being left alone. This could have arisen after his parents' acrimonious divorce, just before his eighteenth birthday and graduation. Due to lack of communication, both parents moved out of the family home at the same time, intending to sell it later. Dahmer's mother took his eleven-year-old brother David with her, and both parents presumed the other was taking care of Dahmer. So when he arrived home from school the house was deserted, the fridge was empty and there was no money to buy food. Although the situation was soon sorted out, it came as quite a shock to Dahmer, with some later commentators suggesting it had a permanent impact on him, making him terrified of abandonment.

Whatever his motivation, once he'd smashed in the hitchhiker's skull he'd got a corpse on his hands. Instead of dealing with it right away, he undressed the body, stroked the dead youth's chest, then masturbated over the corpse, his semen dropping in bursts on to the lifeless flesh.

The next day he was in a state of fear, loathing and panic. He had to get rid of the body. He was only eighteen; he didn't want to spend the rest of his life in jail, not for one rash moment of madness. So he decided to dismember the body. First though, he slit open the stomach and examined the internal organs – this was his way of contemplating his handiwork. Then he cut the body up into manageable pieces and stuffed them into three big bags which he disposed of in an old drainage pipe at the back of the house, covering it with earth.

Once you've killed someone – other than in a legitimate military or police context – there's no going back. You're suddenly different to everyone around you. You become isolated. What's more, there's a very real risk you will kill again, especially if you liked it. And Dahmer did like it, otherwise he wouldn't have masturbated over the corpse.

But Dahmer left it nine years before he killed again. He enrolled at university, but was thrown out shortly afterwards, partly because he had a drink problem. He then served for two years in the army in Germany, at one stage training as a medic (which ironically gave him some handy skills when he took up killing again). His drinking, however, got worse because of the heavily subsidised alcohol available to service personnel, and he was discharged early.

After leaving the army he lived in Florida for a few months before returning to his family in September 1981. He then moved into an apartment owned by his grandmother in West Allis, Wisconsin. His drinking got worse and at one point he was arrested for exposing himself at a state fair, much to the embarrassment of his family who were all churchgoers.

Although he found it difficult to make friends, people seemed to like Dahmer, who was both good-mannered and well-spoken. He wasn't bad looking either – standing six foot tall with dark blonde hair, glasses, and weighing around 190 pounds.

After getting a job on the production line at the Ambrosia Chocolate Company, he started frequenting gay bathhouses in Milwaukee, where he picked up men for sex. But this didn't quite fulfil his needs. He didn't want active sex partners; he wanted them to keep still. 'I trained myself to view people as objects of potential pleasure instead of people, instead of seeing them as complete human beings,' he later said.

He soon thought up a way to keep them still – he slipped sleeping pills in their drinks, rendering them unconscious. He would then fondle them and masturbate himself. Other times he would lay his head on the chest of a man he'd picked up and listen to his heartbeat.

In the end, people started complaining about him and he was banned from using the bathhouses.

The urge to kill came back on 16 November 1987. He was drinking in a Milwaukee gay bar and fell into conversation with Steven Tuomi. The two then rented a room at the Ambassador Hotel, not far away. By this time Dahmer was very drunk and launched a murderous attack on Tuomi, then passed out. He woke up the next morning with a corpse next to him. Tuomi had been strangled to death. In a panic Dahmer rushed out and bought a large suitcase, stuffed Tuomi's body into it, and hauled it back to his grandmother's basement, where he was living, to dispose of it. Before getting rid of the corpse, however, he had sex with it – thrusting his erect penis into the decomposing anus of the body.

Dahmer later said he didn't know what had come over him. 'I couldn't believe it happened again after all those years,' he said. 'I don't know what was going through my mind. I [have] tried to dredge it up, but I have no memory whatsoever.'

This second killing sent him careering down the road to damnation. There was no holding back the dark side of his psyche now. Death, murder and necrophilia became his own holy trinity. And there would be no redemption; he'd got a hard-on for hell and he was going to earn his ticket with more bloodshed and more horror.

Four months later, in January 1988, Dahmer picked up and murdered fourteen-year-old Jamie Doxtator, who hung around the outside of gay bars, desperately looking for love.

Just under three months later, Dahmer took out twenty-three-year-old Richard Guerrero. The next day it was twenty-six-year-old Anthony Sears who, like the others, was drugged, strangled and dismembered – but this time round Dahmer decided to keep the head and genitals as trophies.

Up until now he'd been taking his victims back to the basement flat he rented from his grandmother. Although she lived above she had no idea about his dark activities. But she was well aware of his drinking and the amount of noise he made, all of which became too much for her. So Dahmer rented another apartment in Milwaukee – 213 Oxford Buildings – which gave him the freedom to kill even more regularly.

'For a long time, it was just once every two months,' he said. 'Near the end it was once every week... Just really got completely out of control.'

The killings followed a similar pattern. He would choose a likely candidate in a gay bar or bookshop and engage them in conversation. Being reasonably good looking and articulate he rarely had trouble getting them to go back to his apartment with him, usually on the pretext of watching a video and having a few beers; either that or he'd offer them money to pose for photos. Once there he would spike their drinks with prescription sleeping pills. After his chosen victim had passed out he would strangle them with his belt or bare hands, or would slit their throat with a sharp knife. Then it was time to satisfy his terrifying sexual urges by having sex with the corpse, or masturbating himself over the body.

After that he would begin dissecting the corpse, taking Polaroid photos of the whole process. He wrapped prime cuts like biceps, hearts and thighs in plastic, and preserved the sex organs in formaldehyde. Skulls were boiled clean and painted granite grey. When the mood took him he would line up his growing collection of skulls and masturbate in front of them.

He put what was left of the carcasses in a fifty-five-gallon plastic container filled with acid. This reduced the muscle and bone to a greasy sludge, which was easily flushed down the toilet.

Sometimes he varied his routine. With one victim, for example, he boiled the entire skeleton clean and bleached it. With another he flayed the skin and tanned it like a piece of leather.

To be fair, Dahmer wasn't totally callous about what he was doing; somewhere inside, he recognised it was wrong. But it was a compulsion. 'After the fear and terror of what I had done had left, which took about a month, I started it all over again,' he said. 'From then on it was just a craving, a hunger... And I just kept doing it, doing it, doing it.'

By Dahmer's sixth or seventh victim, things had changed. In a weird kind of way he wanted to become more intimate with his victims and get closer to them. So he turned to cannibalism. 'It started out as experimentation,' he said, 'because it made me feel like they were more part of me.' In a perverse way he was ensuring his lovers – or, rather, his one-night stands – would never abandon him and that he would remain in control of the relationship.

Dahmer told investigators that he ate hearts, livers and thighs. He even bought a special adaptor for his gas stove so he could charbroil the meat, making it more tender. His favourite cut of human meat was the biceps, which he said tasted like 'filet mignon' – the tenderloin cut of beef.

A MATTER OF TASTE

As we've seen, the majority of those who have eaten human meat tend to describe it as tasting like pork (hence the term 'long pig'). But Dahmer said it tasted like beef. So what does it taste like?

Unfortunately the testimonies we have about the taste of human flesh come from people who are not only less than reliable, but are difficult for the ordinary person to relate to. More often than not they are psychopathic killers – or in the case of my cannibal correspondent, Eric Soames, less than balanced. Of course there are those who have eaten human meat in a bid to survive. But again such testimonies are hard for the ordinary person to relate to.

Ideally we would get the lowdown on the taste of human meat from an everyday person.

Clearly, as an investigative journalist, I should be willing to taste some human meat in the interests of research. The only problem is, even though my diet – which is high protein – consists of a lot of animal meat and fish, I personally find the idea of eating human flesh repulsive. It just doesn't seem civilised. I'd eat it if my survival depended on it, of course – in a situation such as the plane crash in the Andes in 1972 when those left alive had no alternative but to resort to cannibalism and – as told in the movie *Alive* – ate the flesh of dead passengers to survive.

But I wouldn't eat human meat out of choice. Luckily, however, one more intrepid than I has already done the job for me – William Bueller Seabrook.

Before we get to the heart – or meat – of the matter, let's briefly look at the kind of man he was, so we can see that his testimony of eating human flesh is likely to be one of the best and most reliable on record.

Seabrook began his career as a reporter and city editor on the *Augusta Chronicle*, Georgia, later becoming a partner in an advertising agency in Atlanta. In 1915, at twenty-nine, he gave it up to join the French army and fight in World War I. He was gassed at Verdun in 1916 (a battle in which a quarter of a million soldiers died). After his medical discharge he was awarded the Croix de Guerre for his courage.

The following year he became a reporter for *The New York Times*. In 1924 he went to Arabia and lived with the Bedouin tribes, chronicling his experiences in *Adventures in Arabia* (1927), which became the first of a string of bestsellers. After that he travelled to Haiti to look into Voodoo and the 'Cult des Mortes', the result of which was his book *Magic Island* (1928).

Seabook's weakness was drink. His alcoholism became such a problem that, shortly before Christmas in 1933, he voluntarily entered a mental institution in Bloomingdale, just outside New York. He remained there until July the following year. He got yet another bestseller out of the experience – *Asylum* (1935).

In his preface to *Asylum* Seabrook points out that his books were not 'fiction or embroidery'. In other words, he walked the talk. So when he turned his attention to cannibalism we can be assured that he was determined no fabrication would be involved.

In 1931, he published *Jungle Ways* which covered a trip he made to West Africa that involved spending time with tribes who still practised cannibalism. In the book he made clear that other authors had evaded the central issue of cannibalism; they remained observers and didn't join in. So how, he asked, could they provide any genuine insight into the practice?

> ...[Other authors] invariably evade the central issue, in the sense that they offer no first-hand observation or experience on the one essential dietetic point that makes the difference between a cannibal and my grandmother. And it seemed impossible, furthermore, for me or anyone to offer anything better unless one actually knew what one was talking about with reference to the precise thing that makes a cannibal a cannibal.

The French writer and explorer Paul Morand (who'd written a preface for the French edition of *Magic Island*) had urged him to go to Africa to resolve the cannibal question, once and for all. He believed Seabrook had the necessary courage needed for the task.

He was able to smooth the way for Seabrook, providing equipment, letters of introduction, and transportation.

Morand felt that the time for such a trip was fast disappearing (cannibal tribes were abandoning the practice), telling Seabrook:

> ...you must try to get inside it. You must see a sacrifice if you can... you must get yourself invited to dinner with the cannibals... no articulate, literate white man has ever done either.

Needless to say, Seabrook was up for it. 'I made up my

mind,' he said, 'before leaving New York that when it came the subject of cannibals I would either write nothing whatever about them, or I would know what I was writing about.'

Not only was he going to walk the talk, he was going to eat the flesh...

Seabrook met members of the Guerú tribe and they agreed that he could join in with their cannibalistic feast. He later admitted to being a little uncomfortable that the human flesh had come from victims speared by Guerú warriors during a raid on another village.

He then asked, 'Why do you eat the flesh of the mammal Homo Sapiens?'

'Why shouldn't we eat it,' came the reply.

Clearly he wasn't going to get far on that line of inquiry. So he asked one of the warriors what parts of human meat were considered best?

The warrior replied that for solid meat the loin cuts, the ribs, and the rump steak were best. The liver, heart, and brains apparently were good as 'titbits', but tasted exactly the same as those of all other animals.

Another warrior said that, as a matter of personal choice, the palm of the hand was the 'most tender and delicious morsel of all'.

One drawback with human meat, Seabrook was told, was that it tended to be tough, and took a great deal of slow cooking to tenderise it (here we might recall Jeffrey Dahmer buying an add-on for his stove that would make the human flesh he consumed more tender).

At that point Seabrook felt duty bound to make the most of it. '[I received] a portion of stew with rice,' he said, 'so highly seasoned with red pepper that fine shades of flavour might be lost to an unaccustomed palate.'

There was a problem, however. The Guerú were suspicious about the white man who had come into their midst. They were worried that word of their cannibalistic ways would get out to the authorities. It turned out that, although Seabrook had seen the victim killed in battle, he was served the meat of an ape, not a man.

He left Africa without achieving his goal. Yet he had vowed he wouldn't write up his experiences if he was not successful.

As it turned out, all was not lost. A solution cropped up in France, where he was staying, which would allow him to write the book:

[A friend] obtained for me from a hospital intern at the Sorbonne a chunk of human meat from the body of the first healthy human carcass killed by accident, that they could dispose of as they chose. I cooked it in Neuilly, at the villa of the Baron Gabriel des Hons, who was my translator. I ate a lot of it in the presence of witnesses.

He recorded the whole thing in minute deal – from the look and feel of the raw meat to cooking it and eating it.

The raw human meat, he said, resembled good beef, but was slightly less red in colour. It was firm in texture and the fat was light yellow like the fat of beef and mutton. The smell was similar to fresh meat from any large domestic animal.

He then grilled the steak, observing that it sizzled and browned like any other meat – and smelled as good. Then came the moment of truth:

I sat down to it with my bottle of wine, a bowl of rice, salt and pepper at hand. I had thought about this and planned it for a long time, and now I was going to do it. I was going to do it, furthermore – I had promised and told myself – with a completely casual, open, and objective mind. But I was soon to discover that I had bluffed and deceived myself a little in pretending so detached an attitude.

It was with, or rather after, the first mouthful, that I discovered there had been an unconscious bravado in me, a small bluff-hidden unconscious dread. For my first despicable reaction – so strong that it took complete precedence over any satisfaction or any fine points of gastronomic shading – was simply a feeling of thankful and immense relief.

At any rate, it was perfectly good to eat! At any rate, it had no weird, startling, or unholy flavour. It was good to eat, and despite all the intelligent, academic detachment with which I had thought I was approaching the experience, my poor cowardly and prejudiced subconscious real-self sighed with relief and patted itself on the back.

I took a big swallow of wine, a helping of rice, and thoughtfully ate half the steak. And as I ate, I knew with increasing certainty what it was like. It was like good, fully developed veal, not young, but not yet beef. It was very definitely like that, and it was not like any other meat I had ever tasted. It was so nearly like good, fully developed veal that I think no person with a palate of ordinary, normal sensitiveness could distinguish it from veal.

It was mild, good meat with no other sharply defined or highly characteristic taste such as for instance, goat, high game, and pork have. The steak was slightly tougher than prime veal, a little stringy, but not too tough or stringy to be inedible. The roast, from which I cut and ate a central slice, was tender, and in colour, texture, smell as well as taste, strengthened my certainty that of all the meats we habitually know, veal is the one meat to which this meat is accurately comparable.

As for any other special taste or odour of a sort which would be surprising and make a person who had tasted it not knowing exclaim, 'What is this?' it had absolutely none. And as for the 'long pig' legend, repeated in a thousand stories and recopied in a hundred books, it was totally, completely false.

It gives me great comfort here to be able to write thus categorically. A small helping of the stew might likewise have been veal stew, but the overabundance of red pepper was such that it conveyed no fine shading to a white palate; so I was glad I had tried it in the simpler ways.

When Seabrook wrote up *Jungle Ways* he simply transferred his genuine experience of eating human meat into his 'cannibal' feast with the Guerú tribe. Like many TV documentary makers today he twisted some key elements and action around to fit the story. Personally I can't see a problem with this. But when the press found out he'd been duped by the Guerú tribe they had a field day and he was laughed at.

The worst of it was he couldn't come clean about how he really had eaten human meat as his supply was obtained illegally.

But not everyone laughed at him:

> Daisy Fellowes [a prominent socialite of the day] came to see me one day with Douglas Fairbanks, Sr., and said, 'It was just too bad, you poor credulous little boy – and with all the trouble you took. I think you deserve to know what human flesh really tastes like, so I am giving you a dinner next week in my garden.

Next week came and dinner was served:

> ...out on the lawn marched the major-domo followed by lackeys in knee-breeches and white gloves, bearing a charcoal brazier, silver dishes, and a platter of meat cut up to be grilled. We ate it and liked it. It looked and tasted exactly like fully developed veal or fine young baby beef. In other words, it looked and tasted exactly like human flesh.

So did Seabrook eat human meat a second time? And was Douglas Fairbanks, Sr. party to cannibalism or was it a huge joke? We'll never know...

KARMA DAHMER

As the killings and cannibalism ran out-of-control Dahmer increasingly came under the thrall of the dark side of his psyche. At one stage he decided to build an altar to the Devil, using his collection of skulls – and the complete skeleton of one of his victims he had now wired together. He became convinced that if he could conjure up the Devil he could persuade him to give him 'special powers and energies to help me socially and financially'.

He was out to make the classic Devil's pact – and he wasn't the first. Indeed the Faustian pact has a long and illustrious history. Legend has it that celebrated blues man Robert Johnson (1911–1938) made a pact with the Devil to gain fame and expertise on the guitar. One night, so the story goes, he went down to a lonely crossroads in the Mississippi Delta, near where he was staying. Out of the darkness came a man, dressed in shabby black top hat and tails, who took Johnson's guitar and tuned it in a special way – to the 'Devil's tuning'. He then gave it back.

After the encounter, Johnson, whose musical output had previously been described as a terrible racket by fellow blues man Son House, became a highly proficient and outstanding guitarist, often moving audiences to tears. He also shot to fame (or at least he became as well known as was possible as an itinerant blues artist in the 1930s), which added fuel to the rumour that he had made a diabolic pact.

When Johnson died young in 1938 (he was still under thirty) people said the Devil had taken his due. There are other possible explanations, of course. For one, some commentators say Johnson was most likely poisoned (his whiskey spiked with strychnine) by a jealous husband whose wife had succumbed to Johnson's notorious womanising.

But the idea that you can make a bargain with the Devil for money and success, or to gain outstanding artistic skills is a persistent one – not just with musicians and other artists, but with murderers like Jeffrey Dahmer too.

He created his shrine to Satan by arranging six skulls on

a long black table, along with the complete skeleton. Then he proceeded to conjure up the Evil One.

It's unlikely the Devil appeared in a puff of sulphurous smoke. But such a ritual would have had a profound impact on Dahmer whose psyche, by now, had lost all grip on reality. Talking about the experience later he revealed that he felt he was being directed by some outside evil force – echoing the feelings of other cannibals we've looked at.

> Am I just an extremely evil person or is it some kind of Satanic influence, or what?... I have to question whether or not there is an evil force in the world and whether or not I have been influenced by it. Is it possible to be influenced by spirit beings? I know it sounds like an easy cop-out... but from all that the Bible says, there are forces that have a[n] influence on people's behaviour. The Bible calls him Satan. I suppose it's possible because it sure seems like some of the thoughts aren't my own, they just come blasting into my head... They do not leave.

Whether Satanic or not, Dahmer's killing spree would never have ended if he hadn't picked up thirty-two-year-old Tracey Edwards who, by some fluke, managed to escape, despite being drugged. He was more formidable than most of Dahmer's victims and succeeded in landing a punch on Dahmer, giving him vital seconds in which to escape and flag down the passing patrol car.

Jeffrey Dahmer's trial began on 17 January 1992 in Milwaukee. Because he'd made a full confession, the issue of his guilt or otherwise was not in question; it was about

230

whether or not he was sane when he committed his crimes.

The security around the Dahmer trial was like nothing ever seen in America. Everyone going into the courthouse was frisked for weapons and scanned electronically. The courtroom was regularly swept for bombs, both electronically and by sniffer dogs. And an eight-foot-high bullet-proof screen was brought in to protect Dahmer from the hordes of people baying for his blood.

A long line of leading psychiatrists testified for both the defence and prosecution. But in the end the jury's verdict was a forgone conclusion. Faced with the gruesome and shocking details of what he'd done – and with the weeping relatives of his victims – it was no surprise when they found him guilty and sane on all seventeen counts of murder.

After being found guilty, he read out a four-page apology to the families of his victims. 'I know how much harm I have caused,' he said. 'Thank God there will be no more harm that I can do... I ask for no consideration.'

He didn't get any. Because Wisconsin didn't have the death penalty he was sentenced to over 957 years in prison, without hope of parole. It was overkill to ensure there would never be any chance of him being released.

After being sentenced, Dahmer added, 'This is the grand finale of a life poorly spent and the end result is just as overwhelmingly depressing... it's just a sick, pathetic, wretched, miserable life story, that's all it is.'

He later said to his lawyer, 'If I was killed in prison, that would be a blessing right now.'

He got his wish.

On November 28, 1994, Dahmer and another inmate named Jesse Anderson were beaten to death by a fellow inmate – schizophrenic killer Christopher Scarver – while on work detail in the prison gym. Dahmer died from severe head trauma in the ambulance while being rushed to hospital.

MARC SAPPINGTON

Two years after Dahmer's death – in 1996 – the city of Milwaukee authorities bought the entire contents of Dahmer's apartment for $400,000 and had them incinerated. They wanted to prevent anyone else from buying them and creating a Jeffrey Dahmer museum. This didn't stop Dahmer's legacy living on, however. He had a disciple whose horrific cannibal killing spree exploded into the news in 2001.

Enter twenty-two-year-old Marc Sappington. Unlike his idol Dahmer, he didn't fit the profile of a serial killer. For a start, the five-foot-eleven 165 pounder, with a rounded face and deep-set brown eyes was black. With one single exception – Wayne Williams, convicted for the Atlanta Child Murders – every known serial killer in American history had been white.

What's more, serial killers almost never begin their killing spree until they are in their thirties (although they might kill one person when they're younger, as Dahmer did); whereas Sappington embarked on his murder spree in his early twenties. He didn't even have much of a police record, just a few minor drug offences; nor did he have a history of sexual violence.

All in all, it would have been hard to have foreseen the bloody carnage he was about to unleash.

No one paid much attention to Marc as he walked along the side streets of Kansas City, Kansas, in March 2001. They should have done. He was looking for victims. In fact, he had no choice. The voices in his head told him that if he didn't kill, they would kill him. 'He feared for his own safety,' said one of the officers who later questioned him.

When he was arrested on 12 April he was the subject of a massive manhunt. Sappington's mother, Mary White, had followed a trail of blood to Marc's room in the basement. To her horror she found bin bags with body parts protruding from them. By the time the police and ambulance arrived she had fallen into a psychotic state – due to the shock and the fact that she had long battled with schizophrenia.

The severed body parts belonged to Alton 'Freddie' Brown, a sixteen-year-old student and friend of Marc who lived with his grandmother, less than a block away. Sappington had blasted him with a shotgun while his back was turned. Using an axe, he then severed his friend's arms at the shoulders and his legs at the knees. Then he sliced off a large chunk of Brown's right calf. He took it upstairs to the kitchen, where he fried it and ate it. After that he went back down to the basement to dismember the body. Every so often, as he chopped up the corpse, he paused to drink some of its blood.

When he was finished, he put Brown's body parts in three green rubbish bags and left them in the basement – an act that proved to be his undoing.

Sappington grew up on the north side of Kansas City, an area plagued by crime, poverty and drug addiction since the 1950s. He lived with his mother Mary White in a run-down, wood-frame house at 1310 Troup Avenue. He never knew his father; he'd left the scene before Marc was born on 9 February 1979.

Mary did her best to keep Marc on the straight and narrow. She was devoutly religious and insisted that Marc go to church with her every Sunday, hoping it would help him to grow into a God-fearing adult. Unfortunately, her mental problems left her unable to work and not always able to take care of Marc as well as she should. Inevitably – and despite singing in the church choir – Marc began to gravitate to the streets.

By the time he entered Wyandotte High School he was drinking heavily and smoking 'dank', a mix of marijuana and PCP (phencyclidine), a powerful and highly addictive hallucinogen, better known as angel dust. Before getting into drugs Marc had been bright, with a quick wit and engaging personality.

By 1996 he'd stopped going to classes, and had also given up attending church.

Dank had become the focus of Marc's life. 'He was heavily into it,' said Eric Finnix, who considered himself Marc's best friend.

He said Sappington loved to smoke his dank and watch TV or a video in the basement, where he spent most of his time.

One time he and Finnix recorded a documentary about Jeffrey Dahmer. It struck a strong chord with Sappington and from that day on he became obsessed with the Wisconsin serial killer and cannibal. He also became obsessed with the movie *Silence of the Lambs* and apparently dreamed of becoming as notorious as the fictional Hannibal Lecter.

Although Dahmer became his idol, Sappington wasn't like him. He didn't prey on homosexuals or bisexuals in gay bars. Nor did he have any inclination to have sex with the corpses of his victims. And besides, three of those he killed were his friends. According to Finnix what he wanted was fame. 'He wanted to go to the pen and be executed and be a legend,' he said. 'He wanted to be the black Jeffrey Dahmer and the black Hannibal Lecter all rolled into one.'

Some kids want to be pop, rock or movie stars or simply celebrities. In a sense Sappington wasn't any different; he just chose the dark route. It was also the easy route as the only work and talent involved is pulling the trigger...

It also came out that Sappington was a fan of snuff movies, a genre of film purporting to depict real-life murders often in combination with bizarre or grotesque sexual scenarios. One of his favourite snuff movies was *Faces of Death*, a series of seven films produced between 1978 and 1996 that show people and animals meeting horrific deaths. While the scenes were either faked or taken from stock footage, they were gruesome and sickening nonetheless. Sappington lapped them up, playing and replaying them on his VCR.

According to the attorney who represented Marc at his trial, he started to show signs of schizophrenia from the age of sixteen. The disabling brain disease that had long afflicted his mother looked like it had been passed on to her son. Although schizophrenia affects both sexes with equal frequency, the disorder often manifests earlier in men than it does in women. With men it usually comes out in their late teens or early twenties; whereas in women it typically appears in their twenties to early thirties.

Clearly, Marc's use of PCP – with its inherent hallucinogenic properties – would have only served to exacerbate any developing mental problems. As it was the drugs and schizophrenia proved to be a deadly combination.

Sappington's first victim had been David Mashak, the newly married owner of a car dealership. On Friday 16 March 2001 Sappington and a friend, sixteen-year-old Armando Gaitan, got hold of an assault rifle and decided to commit an armed robbery. Gaitan reportedly saw it as a way of transforming himself from 'wannabe gangsta' into a real one. His plan didn't include shooting anyone. The idea was for Sappington simply to brandish the weapon while he demanded that cash and other valuables be handed over.

Mashak was chosen at random. He just happened to be alone, busy with paperwork. When the two burst in the door, saying it was a hold-up, he did nothing to resist. Yet Sappington couldn't hold back. He squeezed the trigger, killing Mashak in a hail of bullets.

Gaitan and Sappington hot-tailed out of the dealership. A witness saw them and was able to provide the police with an accurate description of the two raiders.

Gaitan fled out of town. But police soon identified him through a pager he'd left in the dealership. They tracked him down in Texas and brought him back to Kansas City, but he refused to reveal the name of his accomplice.

Meanwhile Sappington's appetite for killing had been whetted. He couldn't wait to kill again. It had given him a sense of power that he'd never felt before. All he needed was to find a suitable victim. As it happened one came to him. Terry Green had planned on going fishing on Friday 6 April. But the weather had turned bad. So he drove over in his Mercury Sable to visit his friend Marc Sappington instead.

As soon as he walked into the basement Marc went for him with a hunting knife. He put up a valiant struggle, but the first wound was deep and he couldn't hold out against Sappington's furious attack. 'It was him or me, so I stabbed him,' Sappington commented later. He chose Green because 'he just happened to come over'.

The murder left pools of blood on the floor of the basement. Marc got down on all fours and lapped at the blood, like a hyena at a carcass.

Thinking neighbours might have heard the disturbance, he wrapped his dead friend's body in a blue canvas sheet, and dragged it out of the basement and loaded it into the Mercury. He then drove four miles to a shopping mall, left the vehicle in the car park and walked home.

No one took any notice of the parked car for three days – not until mall employees noticed the terrible smell coming from it and called the cops.

Three days later Sappington killed again. This time his victim was twenty-two-year-old Michael Weaver, who worked at a dry-cleaners. He was Eric Fennix's step-brother. Sappington had been walking around the streets looking for his next victim, and happened to be outside Weaver's house when he came out on his way to work. They exchanged greetings and Weaver climbed into his Oldsmobile. Before he could close the door, Sappington attacked him from behind, stabbing him in the back with a hunting knife. Although fighting for his life, he managed to speed off, but lost control and crashed into a post.

Sappington ran to the car and got in. He heaved Weaver to the passenger side, then drove the car into a nearby alley, where he left his best friend's step-brother to bleed to death. Before leaving the scene he used his knife to cut away Weaver's bloody t-shirt. He then held it high over his head, squeezed it, and let the blood trickle into his wide open mouth.

Weaver's body wasn't discovered until nine the next morning. Sappington, meanwhile, had become a fully fledged serial killer and was determined to kill again. But this time round he didn't just want to drink his victim's blood, he wanted to eat their flesh.

A few hours after leaving Weaver to die in the alley, Sappington spotted Alton 'Freddie' Brown walking down the street. Brown looked up to Sappington, seeing him as an older brother figure. So when Sappington said, 'Hey, you wanna hang out?', he readily agreed. The houses around Troup Avenue, where Sappington lived, were set back from the road. They were also spaced quite far apart and were surrounded by trees and vegetation. So when Brown turned his back and Sappington pulled the trigger of his twelve-gauge shotgun, no one heard a thing.

No one saw him drag the body into his basement, where he ate a section of Brown's right leg, drank some of his blood, and deposited the remains in three bin bags.

Nothing could have prepared his mother's already shaky psyche for what she found when she entered the basement and saw what her son had done. It drove her mad.

It wasn't a pleasant sight for the police either. 'In my twelve years as a homicide investigator, I'd never seen anything as horrible as this,' said Lieutenant Vince Davenport, commander of the Kansas City Police Department's homicide division, who later interrogated Sappington.

The basement was swimming in blood, with chunks of

flesh strewn across the floor and sticking to the walls and furniture. Opening the rubbish bags was the worst. In one bag were his legs and feet. Another contained his arms and hands. And the third held his torso and head.

By eleven that night a massive manhunt was under way. Off-duty detectives were called out to work on the case, and neighbouring police departments were notified. They eventually caught Sappington during the evening of 12 April, after spotting him on foot at Seventeenth Street and New Jersey Avenue, less than a mile from his home.

He was armed with a pistol, but didn't try to resist arrest when officers confronted him.

Once in custody, Sappington was questioned by Davenport and two plain-clothes officers. They spent over two hours trying one ploy after another, but couldn't get Sappington to talk. Just as Davenport was about to call it a night, Sappington started mumbling something about 'vampires'.

'What did you say, son?' he asked.

'Vampirism, cannibalism,' Sappington muttered.

Once he started, however, he told the investigators everything. He talked about taking drugs and how the voices in his head had threatened to kill him if he didn't do what they said. 'They were telling me I had to eat flesh and blood to live. If I didn't, I would die,' he said.

Davenport later said, 'The really scary thing is that the victims could have been anybody. He talked to me about going out on the street and looking at people, asking the voices in his head "What about him? What about her?" These people never knew that it could have been them, they could have been killed and eaten.'

At one point during his interrogation, Sappington reached

out and grabbed the back of an investigator's thigh and asked, 'Can I have some of that?'

Later, when he was being taken into custody at Wyandotte County Jail, he slapped his hands down on the booking desk and said, 'I'm here, I'm hungry, where's my roommate?' Then he laughed.

Prosecutors filed murder charges against Sappington: three counts of premeditated first-degree murder, punishable by death or life imprisonment with no chance of parole for fifty years on each count.

At a probable cause hearing in January 2002 Sappington's attorney entered a plea of not guilty by reason of insanity.

When the story came out it made headlines around the world. Sappington was famous; or, at least, he'd got his fifteen minutes of fame.

The case finally came to trial on 19 July 2004. By then prosecutors had dropped the death penalty. If he was found guilty, Sappington faced life imprisonment. If he was found not guilty by reason of mental defect he would be remanded to a state hospital for the criminally insane.

As it was, the jury found him guilty on all three counts of murder. During sentencing Sappington apologised for his crimes, telling the judge they were motivated by a 'will to live'. He was clearly referring to the voices in his head threatening to kill him if he didn't do as they instructed and commit murder. This didn't cut any ice with the judge. He looked Sappington straight in the eye and said, 'You are the closest thing to a homicide time bomb. There is no way I am going to endanger the community again.'

With that, he sentenced Sappington to life in prison with

no chance of parole. In September he was put on trial for the murder of David Mashak, his first victim. Sappington had claimed his accomplice Armando Gaitan had been the triggerman. The jury didn't buy it and the judge tacked on another life sentence.

Sappington is currently imprisoned at the El Dorado Correctional Facility in El Dorado, Kansas. Run a search for his name on Google and it returns around 950 results. By no means all are for the serial killer. And those that are consist mainly of press reports from 2001 when the story broke. Marc Sappington's fifteen minutes of fame has clearly long gone. But his victims' families still mourn...

Would Jeffrey Dahmer have been proud of his disciple? Probably not.

VIEW OF THE SHAMAN

And what about the voices in Sappington's head? According to him they instructed him to commit his atrocities – the choice they gave him was: kill or be killed. But the fact was they weren't real. They manifested because of the schizophrenia and the drugs he took. Had he been properly treated for schizophrenia and not taken angel dust... then, just maybe... he'd never have harmed anyone, let alone eaten human flesh.

That's the conventional line given by psychologists, anyway. And I'd go along with it if it wasn't for the fact that some reputable academics have suggested that hallucinogenic drugs can put us into direct contact with non-human entities.

I realise this might sound like I'm going down the line of Eric Soames, my cannibal correspondent, who insisted he was possessed by a demon or 'bad spirit'. But I do think it is worth considering what the ethnobotanist and philosopher Terence McKenna (1946–2000) had to say on the subject of drugs and non-human entities.

During his researches he had taken a wide range of hallucinogenic substances, his favourites being Psilocybin (found in magic mushrooms) and Dimethyltryptamine, or DMT (which it is said makes LSD look like Aspirin).

According to McKenna, DMT opens a doorway into a dimension where one can experience a form of alien intelligence:

> Within ten seconds, you're taken through the chrysanthemum of orange light and into a world where alien entities live – self-transforming machine elves of hyperspace, I call them, self-dribbling basket balls that come bounding up and jump right into you and out again. The amazing thing is that all the time you are exactly who you always were, but you are in their dimension. This is not a hallucination or state of mind. This is real, these entities are real, and they're trying to communicate.

The question is, what if there are evil 'machine elves of hyperspace' that sometimes speak through the minds of people who take drugs and have mental issues?

Before we look further into this, it's worth looking further at McKenna's work to show that he wasn't the oddball he might seem from the above soundbite.

Born in 1946 in Western Colorado, he moved to Los Altos, California, when he was in high school. He graduated from the University of California at Berkeley with a major in shamanism studies and conservation. After some years making a living as a professional butterfly collector, he became co-steward of a botanical garden in Hawaii, where he collected and cultivated endangered psychotropic plant species and their associated lore.

Not surprisingly, his vast storehouse of knowledge of hallucinogens and knowledge of the plants used by shamans in their 'spirit journeys' made him a big attraction on the lecture circuit during the 1980s and 1990s. He became well known around the globe, partly because of his deft one-liners like: 'LSD is a substance that occasionally produces hysteria in people who've never taken it...' Or: 'People ask me if they can achieve the psychedelic state naturally. Sure you can if you're crazy as a shit house owl...'

More seriously, his 1992 book *Food of the Gods* outlined a radical history of drugs and human evolution. He argued that the birth of human consciousness was linked with the use of plant psychedelics by early primates. The Psilocybin mushroom, in particular, he argued, conferred important survival characteristics on them, such as better eyesight, as well as being the motivating force behind the dawn of human consciousness, which set humans apart from other animals.

He contended that by taking hallucinogenic substances, early humans were able to make contact with non-human entities which – although bizarre and not something our modern rationalistic culture could easily relate to – gave them knowledge that transformed early man's consciousness and paved the way for our development as the dominant species on Earth.

Of course, what McKenna said was nothing new. Tribal

shamans have been saying this all along. They take hallucinogenic plants, or use ritual, to make contact with otherworldly beings who help them in many ways – from giving them knowledge about the workings of the universe to assisting with healing or bringing fertility to crops.

But when shamans go on their hallucinogenic journeys they also encounter evil spirits, entities from the dark side. And these – much like in cases of Voodoo possession – can enter the unwary and take them over. The shaman's job is to remove such entities from the psyche of the possessed person.

The key thing about the use of hallucinogens by shamans is they know what they are doing and it is within a cultural and magical context; whereas the average Western hallucinogenic drugs user will simply 'drop acid'. It's no surprise, therefore, that indiscriminate use of such drugs can send users over the edge. And if they happen to have mental problems, then these naturally are going to be made far worse.

But if McKenna, and tribal shamans worldwide, are correct in believing that hallucinogens are a doorway into other realms where non-human entities exist – then couldn't those entities equally make the transition into our world via the same doorway?

Could it be that when Marc Sappington took angel dust a gate was opened in his psyche that let evil entities in which instructed him to kill? Could it be that the voices he heard in his head were real? Could it be that those entities were dark and depraved and liked nothing more than eating the life energies of other sentient beings?

This might sound like something out of science fiction – and be dismissed as nonsense by Western psychologists – but talk to any shaman in a tribal context and they will completely go along with it. They see the world in a different way to Western culture and deal very directly with the 'hidden underlay' that is full of spirits and mythical creatures, all of which are very real to the shaman. What's more, they typically see mental illness as a symptom of spirit possession. And they treat such illnesses as schizophrenia by performing an exorcism.

Many cannibal killers talk of being directed by something 'outside'. Could it be that Western criminologists and psychologists are missing a key aspect in the motivation of cannibal killers? Could it be that these external forces are real – at least in some way?

EPILOGUE:
EXORCISM OF
A CANNIBAL

Towards the end of my talks with Eric Soames, my cannibal correspondent, we talked much about his belief that a demonic entity had been behind his terrifying desire to eat human flesh. I didn't necessarily go along with it. But my philosophy is: neither believe nor disbelieve anything. Which is another way of saying I do my best to keep an open mind at all times.

The idea of spirits and demons, of course, seems primitive and almost embarrassing to our Western rationalistic mindset. But this isn't the case for millions of people around the world – including the Catholic Church – who do believe in such things.

Soames and I also talked much about exorcism, the removing of evil spirits from people, which is performed by everyone from Voodoo priests to exorcists from the Catholic Church.

Eventually he asked if I could arrange an exorcism ceremony for him. He thought it might be the one thing that would bring him relief from his obsession with eating human flesh, which he was currently getting illegally from mortuaries and sometimes graveyards.

I told him I knew just the man for the job. A Canadian shaman called Dr Crazywolf (www.wolfshaman.com). I've known him for some years now. He got in touch with me after reading my book, *Doktor Snake's Voodoo Spellbook* (2004). We hit it off right away and have been in touch ever since.

Crazywolf's roots are in the Ojibwa tribe, which has some fifty thousand members living on reservations in Ontario, Manitoba and Saskatchewan in Canada. Although he's typically referred to as a shaman, Crazywolf dismisses the term as a myth dreamed up by university academics. 'It's more accurate to call me a spirit doctor,' says the six-footer with a long mane of black hair. 'People on the reservations still go to the spirit doctor to help them solve problems in their lives.'

He told me how he uses a 'spirit pot' or 'pot de tête' (a term that reveals a Voodoo influence in his sorcery) to perform sorcery and divination. He puts chicken bones, feathers and herbs in it, then burns them. 'From the smoke I can divine the way the whirlings of fate are impacting a person. I can travel into the spirit world and try to influence the glimmering strands of destiny in their favour.'

Now in his middle-forties, Crazywolf makes a good living doing consultations both for tribal people and everyday Canadians looking to inject spirituality into their lives. He also has clients in other parts of the world – from Europe to Africa.

Every now and then he is called in to perform an exorcism.

'Sometimes people are taken over by bad spirits,' he says. 'Nothing in their life goes right and they change; people around them don't know them no more. So I perform a ceremony to free them from the bad spirit. I make it go away.'

I told him all about Eric Soames and his human flesh eating.

When I had finished, Crazywolf looked very sombre, not his usual jokey self. 'That guy is possessed by a terrible being,' he said. 'The fact that he has never killed anyone shows his spirit is strong. For that reason only I think there is some hope I can help him. But I cannot make guarantees. This is a bad case. I cannot be certain I can win against such a creature. But I will try.'

I contacted Soames and he agreed to pay Crazywolf his usual fee, plus expenses – which Soames promptly transferred via Paypal (whether the transaction 'exorcising a cannibal' was a first for them, I don't know).

A date was set for Crazywolf to fly over. All we needed then was a location. Crazywolf said the exorcism would ideally be performed at a 'place of power', such as a stone circle. Clearly going to somewhere like Avebury Circle in Wiltshire or the Rollright Stones in Oxfordshire would have drawn too much attention, and may well have led to us being arrested – which would have been a disaster all round.

After much thought I decided on the Gog Magog Hills, a range of chalk hills running several miles to the south-east of Cambridge. The dowser and archaeologist Tom Lethbridge claimed to have found some ancient figures buried in the chalk under the surface of the hills. These, he said, represented a sun god, moon goddess and warrior god. This suggested the area was probably considered sacred in ancient times, and so it fitted the bill as a 'place of power'.

The other good thing about the location was it lay halfway between me in Norwich and Soames in London.

A few weeks later Crazywolf arrived from Canada. He stayed with me for a few days before we set off to do the exorcism ceremony. During that time we talked about the chances of curing Soames' condition.

'The bad spirit has been in him for a long time,' said Crazywolf, 'so it won't be easy to extract it. I'll have a fight on my hands.'

He went on to relate how he'd had some dealings with cannibals before, on a trip to Africa during summer 2006. He'd been shocked to discover two traditional healers were eating flesh.

'They were a husband and wife team based in Mozambique,' he said. 'They'd been digging up corpses to eat the flesh and powdered bones.'

Apparently the two – Neva Mafunga (fifty) and Nhanvura Faera (thirty-four) – had been caught in possession of human organs. Crazywolf had been brought in as an advisor due to his detailed knowledge of traditional healing.

'They said eating human flesh strengthened their power to heal people,' Crazywolf said. 'But it was dark, baleful sorcery fit only for the lowest, left-hand orders of witchcraft.'

Belief in the power of witchcraft in the region is prevalent, but according to police, cases of cannibalism are rare.

The husband – Neva Mafunga – confessed to tucking into human fare for over twenty years, but his wife said she'd only done it on his instructions.

The question was, had they killed people to get the flesh they craved? Or had they feasted on already dead bodies?

Crazywolf said, 'It couldn't be proven that they had murdered anyone for flesh.' But went on to say that, irrespective of the legalities of cannibalism, there's actually a level of risk to health associated with it.

For example, the Fore tribe in Papua New Guinea, who continued to practise cannibalism up until the 1950s, found this out to their cost. While the men of the tribe used to supplement their bean and sweet potato diets by eating small animals, the women and children made up for lack of protein by eating the brains of tribal members who had recently died.

'They ended up dying from brain disease,' said Crazywolf.

According to scientists the symptoms were similar to the human form of mad cow disease. Although the jury is out as to the exact cause, experts speculate that the deaths could well have resulted from the consumption of human brains.

I thought about that for a moment, then remarked to Crazywolf, 'If there was any justice in the world, psychopathic cannibal killers like Issei Sagawa would have contracted something similar. At least then the families and friends of their victims might feel they had got their just desserts, if you'll pardon the pun, rather than getting off lightly for their horrific crimes.'

I remembered another cannibal killer who had been given an incredibly light sentence during the late 1990s. This was David Harker who said he strangled mother-of-four Julie Paterson with her tights after he 'got bored' during a sex session. He then had sex with her corpse before chopping off her head and limbs.

His ugly desire satiated, he began to feel peckish. So he sliced some flesh from her thigh, skinned it, and cooked it with pasta and cheese sauce.

Harker – who had 'Subhuman' and 'Disorder' tattooed on his scalp – then dumped thirty-two-year-old Julie's torso in a bin liner not far from her bedsit.

After his capture, psychologists concluded he was 'an extremely dangerous individual who had shown no remorse'. Tests revealed he was in the top four per cent of the most disturbed psychopaths. He freely admitted to doctors that he had erotic fantasies about mutilating bodies.

Harker was sentenced to fourteen years in prison before he could be considered for parole. Considering his victim had four children, you could hardly describe his punishment as severe.

As Crazywolf commented, 'You can't let people like that loose on society – it's a given they'll kill again. It doesn't matter what is driving them – a demon or derangement – once they've killed and tasted their first blood there is no stopping them.'

He believed that there was hope for Eric Soames because he hadn't yet killed. He hadn't wholly given in to the terrible force that was driving him.

It was a hot weekend in Summer 2007 when Crazywolf and I prepared to set off for the exorcism ceremony. He loaded my car with the various ritual tools he needed, which included his tribal robes and an intricately decorated staff.

Before we left, my wife Nicky – who is something of a sceptic – said, 'Don't you think you're on the wrong track here? Don't you think you should consider the psychological angle more? All the cannibal killers you're featuring in you book had pretty loveless upbringings. I think this is a major factor. They didn't get any love so became cold and detached themselves.

This would have made it easier for them to kill. And in the case of this guy Eric Soames, it would have made it easier for him to eat human flesh which, after all, is the last taboo.'

She had a point. But there was no turning back for us now. We had to see this ugly assignment through to the end.

It took a couple of hours for us to get to Cambridge, via the A11 from Norwich. We then took the bypass towards Cherry Hinton and the Gog Magog Hills. We'd agreed to meet Soames in a more remote part of the Gog Magogs. So we had to leave the car in a public car park, used mostly by ramblers, and make our way on foot using an Ordnance Survey map. Soames had said he would do the same.

It was about 8pm and beginning to get dark when we found Soames waiting on the desolate hillock where we said we'd meet. Despite his dark tastes he looked very ordinary. He was in his late fifties, had greying short hair and wore rectangular metal-rimmed spectacles. He looked quite fit and muscular – which he later said was down to his love of hiking and country walks.

Soames was well-spoken, but this was no surprise as his parents had been middle-class professionals.

'Ah, Jimmy and Crazywolf, nice to meet you both,' he said, offering his hand to me, then Crazywolf, to shake.

'Good to meet you too, after all the time we spent talking by email!' I said.

With the formalities out of the way, it was time to get down to business.

Crazywolf began setting up his ceremonial circle ready to perform what he called the 'Ritual of the Four Divine Winds'.

He collected some large stones to mark the four compass

directions on the perimeter of the circle. He also put a stone in the centre, which he said would be the altar stone. He then sprinkled red powder paint all around the edge of the circle.

After that he gathered together a large bunch of sticks and fallen branches and built three 'sacred fires' inside the circle. My job was to keep these alight during the ceremony.

Once everything was ready – and Soames had put on his ceremonial robes – he directed Soames to lie down in the centre of the circle, close to the altar stone. 'Take your glasses off,' he instructed, 'so you don't hurt yourself.' Not surprisingly Soames began to look very nervous about what was to come.

Crazywolf opened the ceremony by raising his arms to the skies, declaring, 'I call upon the great teacher and divine father Kitchie Manito! I call Wabununk-Daci, powerful spirit of the East! I call Cawnunk-Daci, guardian of the southern gates! I call on Ningabian-Daci, walker of the western lands! I call upon Kiwedinunk-Daci, spirit of the northern wastes! By the prophet's pole of ancient lore let the ritual begin!'

Crazywolf started a slow dance around the sacred fires, muttering a hypnotic song to his ancestors. After about ten minutes of doing this the atmosphere began to change and became heavy and eerie. It felt as if an ancient presence had entered the circle.

Then without warning, Crazywolf shrieked and crouched down next to Soames, who now looked nothing short of terrified. He looked Soames directly in the eyes and shouted, 'I'm talking to the spirit now... You must leave, leave, LEAVE! Get out! Ugly brute of a spirit. Begone and find another home!'

This went on for some considerable time, shattering the silence of the lonely hillock.

Soames meanwhile was shaking uncontrollably, almost as if he was having an epileptic fit. I started to worry that he might die – an occurrence I really wouldn't have wanted to explain to the police. I started to say something to Crazywolf, but he motioned me to be quiet and told me to see to the sacred fires.

Eventually Crazywolf's chants and Soames' shaking reached a terrifying climax, with Soames suddenly letting out a shrill, yet mournful cry – one I shall never forget for its strange mix of sadness and ugliness.

Crazywolf collapsed on the floor, exhausted. I went over with a bottle of mineral water and sprinkled some over his face, which brought him round.

'It's done,' he said. 'The spirit has left him. For a second I thought I was going to lose.'

I looked round at Soames. He'd stopped shaking and was getting up. He looked very white, and yet looked strangely tranquil and at peace.

'It's gone...' he whispered. Then looking at Crazywolf, he said, 'You've saved my soul.'

After we'd packed everything up and made sure the fires were out, we left for a village pub. None of us said very much. The experience had drained us. But Soames humbly thanked Crazywolf and said he knew for sure his cannibalistic urges were gone forever.

I never heard from Soames again after that. I think he didn't want to burden me. Being an honourable sort of chap I'd say he recognised that few people would want a cannibal – albeit a reformed one – as a friend or correspondent. And the truth is he's right.

FURTHER READING

(All other sources are cited in the text)

Boar, Roger and Blundell, Nigel. *The World's Most Infamous Murders*. Hamlyn Publishing, 1990.

Constantine, Nathan. *A History of Cannibalism*. Arcturus, 2006.

Davidson, Peter. *Death By Cannibal*. Berkley Books, 2006.

Davis, Carol Anne. *Sadistic Killers*. Summersdale, 2007.

Donnelly, Mark and Diehl, Daniel. *Eat Thy Neighbour*. Sutton Publishing, 2006.

Dunning, John. *Strange Deaths*. Arrow Books, 1987.

Dunning, John. *Occult Murders*. Senate Press, 1997.

Green, Miranda Aldous. *Dying for the Gods*. Tempus Publishing, 2002.

Haddon, Alfred C. *Magic and Fetishism*. Constable and Company, 1921.

Havill, Adrian. *Born Evil: A True Story of Cannibalism and Serial Murder*. St Martin's Press, 2001.

Heimer, Mel. *The Cannibal: The Case of Albert Fish*. Xanadu, 1971.

Holmes, Ronald, *The Legend of Sawney Bean*. Frederick Muller, 1975.

Jones, Lois. *Cannibal*. Berkley, 2005.

Korn, Daniel and Radice, Mark and Hawes, Charlie. *Cannibal: The History of People-Eaters*. Channel 4 Books, 2001.

Lee, Sandra. *Kathy the Cannibal*. John Blake, 2004.

Leyton, Elliot. *Hunting Humans: The Rise of the Modern Multiple Murderer*. Penguin, 1986.

Marriner, Brian. *Cannibalism: The Last Taboo*. Arrow Books, 1992.

Martingale, Moira. *Cannibal Killers: The History of Impossible Murders*. Carroll & Graf, 1993.

Wilson, Colin. *The Misfits: A Study of Sexual Outsiders*. Grafton Books, 1988.

Wilson, Colin and Wilson, Damon. *World Famous Serial Killers*. Magpie Books, 2005